MW00983587

"This is a story about a powerful love between two people, as well as a story about how universal love can transcend time, borders, and differences. What a beautiful reminder that we are all here simply to love."

Marci Shimoff, bestselling author of *Happy For No Reason*

"If you are ready to have your heart broken open to love and learn profound lessons that will impact and transform every relationship in your life, curl up with *Love Unfiltered*."

Marcia Wieder, Founder, Dream University

"Margot, Amanda, and Mike—I wanted to get to know each of these wonderful individuals and say 'thank you' for demonstrating that we have an astonishing capacity for love. *Love Unfiltered* talks straight from the heart with compassion, wisdom, and courage."

Charles Garfield, Ph.D., Founder, Shanti Project, Author of *Sometimes My Heart Goes Numb: Love and Caregiving in a Time of AIDS*

"In *Love Unfiltered*, Mike Murphy teaches, through his very personal sharing, how to bring your dreams into fruition, whether you are at the top or the bottom of the heap. Mike is phenomenal at taking a vast amount of information, from many sources, and making it simple, practical, and reachable for the average person. He is the real deal. He is not some robed guru, get-rich-quick author, or intellectual psychologist. Mike is a guy who came from the trenches and now teaches with an uncanny sense of being able to meet you just where you are."

Dr. Lee Jampolsky, bestselling author of *Healing the Addictive Personality*

"Mike Murphy's book is a rare coming together of the inspirational and the practical. The tools to truly change your life are here. Mike's journey from the troubled young man that he was to the wise and compassionate man that he is will move you to trust the power of love if you let it."

Dale Borglum, Executive Director of the Living/Dying Project

"With great honesty, Mike Murphy compellingly shares his personal journey and the lessons he learned about the timeless power of love, humility, and compassion. Margot's care and love for others is evident in the story and lives on strongly today through the selfless services supported by the foundation Mike started in her memory."

Kaushik Roy,
Executive Director, Shanti Project

Love
Unfiltered

To Margot—
If only I knew then what I know now, we would
have had it all—but perhaps we did and we
still do.
Together, wherever, forever, I love you, honey

. . .

To anyone who has ever longed for more, lost
at love, struggled to find purpose, and wanted
to give up but never did, this book is written for
and dedicated to you.

Unfiltered

MICHAEL MURPHY

NEXT CENTURY
PUBLISHING

Love Unfiltered

Copyright ©2014 by Michael Murphy
All rights reserved.

Published by Next Century Publishing
www.NextCenturyPublishing.com

No part of this publication may be reproduced, stored in a retrieval system, or transmitted in any form or by any means—electronic, mechanical, photocopy, recording, or any other—without the prior permission of the author.

ISBN: 978-162-9039060

Printed in the United States of America

LOVE UNFILTERED

How to Triumph over Tragedy, Find Your Purpose & Live Your Dreams

Michael Murphy
Founder of the Love From Margot Foundation

**To contact the author about speaking or
appearances simply email:
mike@mikemurphyunfiltered.com**

Acknowledgement

Like the life that inspired it, this book could not have come into being without the support of many people, both personal and professional. First and foremost, for her partnership in the creative process, I want to thank Ellen Daly, who continues to amaze me with her deep insights that come from such a quiet inner well of brilliance. My gratitude also goes to my sister Dana, who lent her editorial skills to this and other books; to Dr. Lee Jampolsky, who read the manuscript and provided feedback; to Marcia Wieder, who gave invaluable advice and support; and to my dear friend Dale Borglum, who was there for me in my darkest days—I will always be grateful for that and for the many edits that he performed on this book. Also, thank you to Sarah Bryant, whose hard work and dedication has helped make both this book and the Love From Margot Foundation successful realities.

I could not have reached the place where I could write this book without my amazing family. Words cannot express how much I owe to my children, Michelle, Michael, Christopher, and Kelli—your love and support inspired me to keep going when I didn't want to try anymore. And to Lisa, who gave me the greatest gift a woman can give a man in these four amazing children. I am also grateful to Martha—I will never forget the way you loved and cared for your daughter in the darkest of days, and how deeply Margot loved you. Those moments will always inspire me to do a little more. My heartfelt thanks go also to my mother—without your love I

13

would be living under a freeway somewhere or worse. To my grandfather, who taught me the power of having a foundation based on integrity and that reputation is everything. To my father, who taught me an incredible work ethic and that if you are going to do something you should do your best, 100 percent of the time, or don't do it at all. To Paco, who fights bravely every day with such a positive attitude—you were Margot's hero. To Lola— every year you become more beautiful and stronger, and I can feel your sister's pride. To Brian—your growth in business and fatherhood I greatly admire. To my sister Stacy—thanks for being there for both of us. To my brothers Bob and Jim, for all of your support. To my grandchildren, Sailor, Hudson and Sutton—so much is riding on you and your generation to grow this concept of love and service. No matter where I am, I will be rooting for you. This also goes for my many nieces and nephews.

To all of our many friends and family who supported Margot and me with your love, compassion, and so many random acts of kindness, I love you and thank you from my total being. And to all of those people we never met or have yet to meet who inspired us along our journey, thank you so much.

To all of our clients at the Love From Margot Foundation, you inspire me with your courage and grace as you rise above life's challenges with limited resources while maintaining such grace. I consider it an honor and a privilege to be involved in your recovery.

Table of Contents

PROLOGUE

Margot's Gift

My wife Margot loved to chase sunsets. In Arizona, I remember clinging to the side of her golf cart as we careened across the rocky ground, following the last rays of light until we topped a rise and were blinded by the beauty of the desert evening. On vacation in Hawaii, she grabbed my hand and

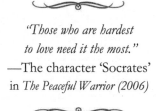

"Those who are hardest to love need it the most."
—The character 'Socrates' in *The Peaceful Warrior (2006)*

scrambled barefoot to the highest point on the island to catch the last fleeting glimpse of crimson glory before it sank beyond the horizon. I will never forget her face, the flush of exertion deepened by the rosy light of the setting sun, and our laughing with joy that we had reached the top in time to watch it slowly sink into dusk.

Margot's life was like one of those sunsets—beautiful but fleeting, flooding the world around her with love and light even as she slipped away too soon. When her doctors told her that the cancer she had been fighting for most of the ten years I'd known her had spread to her spinal fluid and her brain, and that she would die in six weeks without treatment, or in six months if she chose treatment, we didn't even pause to think. We clasped hands and scrambled for higher ground, stretching out the beauty of her life for six more months, even though she endured more suffering than I could have imagined possible. It wasn't because she was afraid to die that she chose to fight—it was because she loved life so much.

Some people are born into this world with unusual gifts—for music, for invention, for physical feats or mental brilliance. Margot's gift was her ability to love. She loved more fully than anyone I've ever met. Her love found its way through my own toughest defenses— catching me off-guard with an unexpected note in my lunch bag or a reminder that she loved me programmed into my phone that showed up just at the moment I was doubting or fearful. In those final months she became even more radiant, lifted beyond the suffering of her body into a state of luminous love that only grew stronger as she grew weaker.

When I gave the eulogy at her memorial—the hardest speech I have ever given—I simply listed all of the people she had loved and the ways in which her love had transformed their lives. As I came to the end, looking around the church at the sea of faces softened by love and grief, I said, "And here comes the hard part— the part that doesn't really go with the rest. She loved me. Why me?"

It really was, and continues to be, a mystery to me. Why did this extraordinary woman, this vibrant, beautiful, earthly angel, fall in love with me—a messed-up, selfish, defensive and emotionally unavailable guy more than fifteen years her senior? I can't explain it. But she did. And that gift—her relentless love, unfiltered by fear or mistrust—broke me down and opened me up until I finally became someone who could give.

I didn't learn easily. My fear, my childhood demons, my carefully constructed defenses all conspired to protect me from the gift she had to give. At times, I wasn't able to fully appreciate what she was holding out to me. Other times, I would destroy it with my guilt and fear. But she persevered in loving me despite myself and slowly but surely broke down my walls.

I've always known I would write a personal-growth book one day to give back to the world just a little of the strength and motivation I've received from the thousands of inspirational books I've read over the past few decades. Each book has been like a life preserver thrown to me as I was tossed on the seas of life, a small raft to carry me for a while before a wave would wrest it from my grip, sucking me under for a while until the next piece of life-saving wisdom would appear. I used to think that the title of my book would be *Three Steps Forward and Two Steps Back*, for that is how I have lived most of my life. Thanks to Margot, however, I finally learned how to avoid self-sabotage. I learned more from her life—and her death—than I have from all the personal-development books I've read over the years. And her example changed the way I understood some of the most powerful lessons I'd learned from the many teachers I met on my journey. It is that wisdom that I hope to share with you in this book—the wisdom of love unfiltered by fear.

No matter where you are coming from, what mistakes you have made, how you have failed or stumbled on your path, you will not find judgment from me in these pages. I have known the path of fear and guilt and regret. I have not felt deserving of the gift I was given. As I said at her memorial, I don't know why she loved me. But because she did, and I was finally able to let it in even after she left this world, I feel blessed to be here and able to share her love with you.

This book is Margot's gift—to me, and through me, to you, the reader. I was given the greatest gift any human being can receive—the gift of love. Margot taught me the power of love, unfiltered—love without any hesitation or constraint. She taught me what love means and how it can heal. And the greatest lesson she taught me is that love prevails. Love doesn't die. It may appear elusive, fragile, impermanent, but it is none of these things. We can banish it, lose it, bury it with our guilt and fear, but it remains unbroken. Like the setting sun, it may seem to sink below the horizon, as it did for me when she died, but in fact, it rises again, even more glorious, with the new day.

Less than two years after Margot died, I found myself sitting at another deathbed. Amanda, the young woman who lay there, struggling to breathe, was the same age as my wife had been, and she had been struck down by the same disease, but little else in her circumstances resembled Margot's. Through my becoming her friend and helping to give her access to the treatments she needed but could not afford, my journey had come full circle.

Margot's life taught me that love is real. Her death taught me that love is eternal. Amanda's death taught me that love is infinite, and that its only purpose is to be given, and amplified, in the process. Margot's death broke me open, but Amanda's death filled my now-open heart with a passionate sense of purpose and unconditional love. I had found my calling, and my life since then has been dedicated to sharing with others the gift of love that I found through these two tragic deaths. I learned love's lessons the hard way, but I am grateful beyond measure to be able to share them now with my readers.

Love is a Promise that Must Be Kept

It was a summer evening, and I was standing on the deck outside my beautiful multi-million-dollar hilltop home, looking down across my five acres of land to the valley below. Mount Diablo rose in the distance behind me, and ahead, the sun was setting over the distant waters of San Francisco Bay. Through the open windows, I could hear the laughter of my four children, and my wife's warm voice calling them to come down for dinner.

"Some people don't understand the promises they're making when they make them," I said . . . "Right, of course. But you keep the promise anyway. That's what love is. Love is keeping the promise anyway."

—John Green,
The Fault in Our Stars

It was as close to perfect as I could have asked for. Two decades earlier, if someone had told me I would end up living a life like this, I'd have just laughed at the absurdity of such a thought. Who was I to even hope for such abundance? And yet now, as I stood there like a king surveying my kingdom, one thought

23

crowded out everything else in my mind: "What are you doing with your life?"

I had everything I wanted, but I wasn't happy. I loved my family immensely, I enjoyed the beauty of our home and the comforts and pleasures that my substantial income afforded us. But I felt strangely lost—like I'd wandered off the road somewhere along the way and found myself in this beautiful place, but in the process I'd forgotten where I was supposed to be going. Well, that's not quite true. I hadn't entirely forgotten. Somewhere, just on the edge of my awareness, I knew why. I'd been trying to push away that nagging feeling for years, but it was always there, hovering in the background: a broken promise. I had made a promise, back when I had nothing. I had everything now, and I still hadn't made good on it.

What was that promise? It was simple—I had promised to give back. The universe had kept its promise to me, ten times over—lifting me from a life of brokenness, addiction, loneliness, and pain to one of health, wealth, abundance, and love. But I hadn't kept my side of the bargain. I had not used my good fortune to help others less fortunate than me as I had vowed I would. And so the universe was teaching me the most profound lesson of my life so far: that *love is a promise that must be kept.*

I had thought of love as something to get—something I needed to have for myself. For a kid who had grown up so starved for love and affection, it's an understandable mistake. I didn't realize that love can't be "had," it can only be received with an open heart and then allowed to flow out, amplified, to embrace others.

24

Love is not just a human emotion—it is the essence of the universe, the energy and power that animates and connects everything. Some people like to use the word "God" to describe this power, and I'm comfortable with that term, but if you prefer to stay away from religious language, you can simply see it as universal love. The universe showered me with love when I asked for it, and my promise had been to give love in return, to those who needed it most. But I hadn't done so. I'd retreated to my hilltop with my family, my wealth, and my security, trying to protect the love I'd gained, and I'd pushed that promise to the back of my mind.

This is not a cautionary tale designed to convince you that achieving wealth and success is meaningless. Far from it. Wealth and success are wonderful things, not least because if you are wealthy and successful you will have more money and energy to give. And this book will teach you how to bring all of that into your life in abundance. That's the good news: the universe is made of love, and if you learn how to tap into that energy, you really can have anything you want. What I will be sharing is not new or original—these are principles that all the great teachers of personal development have shared. But I hope that hearing it through the lens of my particular story will help you understand and relate to these principles. In this chapter, I'll tell you about how they worked for me—how I went from being an uneducated juvenile delinquent with a drinking problem to being a healthy, wealthy business owner with a beautiful home and a wonderful family. I don't regret having brought any of that into my life, and I want you to experience that abundance as well.

But I also want to share with you the even better news: that when you learn to give back that love, that abundance, you will experience a happiness and fulfillment that no amount of riches or achievements alone can give you. When you keep the promise of love, you discover purpose. So it's a win-win! You can have everything you ever wanted *and* find your purpose in life, and there will be more love in the universe. In the next chapter, I'll help you get clear about your own dreams and manifest them in a way that includes the critical fulfillment of love's promise: the element of giving back. That way, you can avoid the mistake I made and go straight to the win-win.

You Can Get There from Here

No matter where you are in life right now, I'm here to show you how you can have everything you ever wanted—and more. If you feel like everything's going in the wrong direction, take a deep breath and stop. I've been there. It feels like you're being sucked down a drain with nothing to grab hold of. But this is the moment you can turn it all around. It doesn't matter how tough things seem, how badly you've messed up, how many bridges you've burned or hearts you've broken, including your own. It's not too late to repair the damage and succeed beyond your wildest dreams. If you feel like your life's not that bad, but you're just flat-lining, not really going anywhere, I can show you how to break out of the numbness and let the energy of love propel you forward. If your life has been pretty good up until now—if you've been blessed with a supportive family, a good education, and some degree of success—then I will simply suggest ways to accelerate your journey. And if you've been successful beyond your wildest dreams but find yourself, as I did, feeling unhappy and unfulfilled, I can help you to discover the missing piece that will make all of it meaningful. I've come to believe that there is an unimaginable power within each and every one of us. For some, it may seem like only a tiny, flickering flame, almost snuffed out by the negativity in the world around us and the limiting beliefs in our own minds. But my goal in this book is to fan this flame, to make it bright and strong and powerful so that it radiates through you in everything you do. I'd like to share my story with you, because if I can get there from where I was, you can get there from here, whatever "here" looks like for you.

My dad's parents were both alcoholics, and he was made a ward of the state of California at the age of thirteen. Sure enough, he grew up to become an alcoholic himself, and my mother, although sweet and loving, was unable to do anything but support his habit. There's a photo in one of our family albums of me, a one-year-old, with a bottle of beer wedged between my chubby knees and a cigarette hanging out of my mouth. I'm sure it was just a joke on my parents' part, but unfortunately it was prescient. I started drinking in eighth grade, spent my teenage years in and out of jail, and was kicked out of three schools. Between the ages of sixteen and eighteen, I survived eight car accidents, all of them alcohol-related. At the age of fourteen, I ran away from home, traveling from Cincinnati, Ohio, to Lexington, Kentucky, with just a few dollars in my pocket, staying in Lexington a few weeks before a kind priest helped me find my way home. That was the first of a number of attempts to leave it all behind.

In my early twenties, I married Lisa, my teenage sweetheart. It was a drunken, spur-of-the moment decision on my part that threw together two lost and lonely young people who didn't really know themselves or each other that well. I was a terrible husband— unfaithful, eventually unemployed, and fast adopting my father's worst habits as I drank and did drugs to dull my guilt over the disaster I was making of my marriage. Lisa became pregnant, and when my daughter Michelle was just two months old, I looked at myself in the mirror and was overwhelmed by shame and humiliation at what a loser I'd become, and the fact that everyone knew it. So I ran away from it all, just as I had as a teenager and many times since. Only this time, Lisa had had enough. When I called her after a week of partying, she refused to take me back.

Driving aimlessly through town, I ended up at the church where we had gotten married. I wasn't a believer, but I was so desperate that I stumbled up the steps of the church, only to find the door locked. So I sat out on those steps and demanded that if God was real, he should manifest right there—then, and only then, would I believe and change my ways. But nothing happened.

"When you get into a tight place and everything goes against you, till it seems as though you couldn't hold on a minute longer, never give up then, for that's just the place and time that the tide'll turn."

—Harriet Beecher Stowe, *Old Town Folks*

28

The Mystery Man

By the spring of 1983, I was divorced and felt like I was dying inside, although I would never admit that to anyone. I had made a resolution to turn my life around, whatever it took, but I honestly didn't know if I could survive the pain in the meantime. I put on a tough face, got a job waiting tables, and dutifully fulfilled my child-support obligations. I joined a program and stopped drinking. I started reading every self-help book I could get my hands on. But the noose around my heart grew tighter and tighter the harder I tried to break through. I was living in a constant state of fear and depression. In hindsight, I think I was experiencing the accumulated pain of all my childhood wounds, but most immediately, the source of my anguish was my separation from my wife and infant daughter.

It was all my fault. That was the worst part. I had created this mess, and now I had to survive long enough to fix it. At one of my lowest moments, a good friend introduced me to a man who he thought could help me. Strangely, neither my friend nor I can recall the man's name all these years later, but I remember every detail of the time I spent with him, because he completely changed my life.

I arrived at his house in a 1971 Ford Pinto that my friend had loaned me. Although it was a cold and rainy Northern California day, I had to keep the car window open because the driver door had been damaged by another car one night as I slept and now did not stay closed unless I drove with one arm out of the window, holding the door shut. I pulled up outside the modest home of this mystery man with one wet arm and wildly disheveled hair.

My friend had told me that this man would help me, but it would cost me $50 an hour, an awful lot of money to me at the time. I barely scraped by on the $2,000 a month I made waiting tables at two different restaurants, and I was $40,000 in debt. But I was desperate, so I took a deep breath, scraped my wet hair off my face, and rang the doorbell.

An unremarkable-looking middle-aged man answered and invited me in. I'll call him John for the sake of the story, as I honestly cannot remember his name. He explained that we would meet one hour a week for seven weeks, and between our meetings I would do just a little work to prepare for the next. In the seventh week, he told me, I would receive a gift that would forever change my life. He said it with so much passion that it scared me. Leaning in close so his face was almost touching mine, he shouted, "You do this and you will get everything you want!"

Shrinking back in my chair, all I could think about was the $350 that I didn't have. I also noted the worn furniture and bad condition of the house, which did not give me much confidence in this man's ability to materialize anything. Plus, it all just seemed a bit farfetched. These days, since the success of the film *The Secret,* the idea of manifestation has become much more widely recognized and understood. In fact, it's a "secret" that certain rare human beings have known about for a long time. Back then, though, it wasn't something people talked about that much, so I was understandably skeptical. I had nowhere else to turn, however, and I remembered how one of the inspirational authors I'd been reading said that when you spend money on your mind, it is not an expense but an investment. No one had ever invested in my mind, so I figured I'd take a chance and see if it paid off. Besides, if I didn't like the first week, I wouldn't return, so I would only be down $50. This was how I justified it to myself, but I knew deep down that it wasn't really about my mind. It was about the unrelenting pain in my heart. I scribbled out a check.

What I learned that day is that the fundamental essence of the universe is energy. That may sound like an esoteric concept, but more than a few respected scientists have come to a similar conclusion. Max Planck, a Nobel Prize–winning German physicist and contemporary of Einstein, who many consider to be the father of quantum theory, wrote the following:

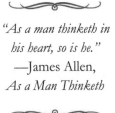

"As a man thinketh in his heart, so is he."
—James Allen,
As a Man Thinketh

> As a man who has devoted his whole life to the most clear-headed science, to the study of matter, I can tell you as a result of my research about atoms this much: There is no matter as such. All matter originates and exists only by virtue of a force which brings the particle of an atom to vibration and holds this most minute solar system of the atom together. We must assume behind this force the existence of a conscious and intelligent mind. This mind is the matrix of all matter.[1]

Contemporary quantum physicists will tell us much the same—while they may use more complex terms, the essential message is simple: the fundamental element of reality is not matter, but energy. If you're interested in what science has to say on the subject, you can certainly find backup for this statement. But for the purposes of this book, I will leave it to that simple statement and add one further clarification that the scientists might not feel is within the scope of their expertise to declare: the nature of that energy is love.

What does all this have to do with manifesting your heart's desires? If everything in the universe is energy, then the "things" we want are more like currents of energy that we simply need to figure out how to redirect toward us. How do we direct energy? Through the power of our attention and our thoughts. There is a common phrase that captures this succinctly: *Where attention goes, energy flows.* The famous early-twentieth-century author Napoleon Hill knew this secret, which he learned from his mentor, Andrew Carnegie. That's why he entitled his bestselling book *Think and Grow Rich*, and he taught millions of readers that, "Whatever the mind can conceive and believe, it can achieve." Prentice Mulford, a contemporary of Ralph Waldo Emerson, wrote a book called *Thoughts Are Things,* in which he described thought as "the unseen magnet, ever attracting its correspondence in things seen and tangible."[2]

This image of thought as a magnet is a popular one today, used by teachers of "the law of attraction," who explain that what you think about is what you attract into your life. Thoughts are things, so be careful about what you think. There's a little more subtlety to this principle, however, as John the mystery man explained to me during that first meeting in his living room. It's all very well to say, "Okay, I'm just going to think positive thoughts now," but the problem is that most of the thinking we do is happening below the surface of our conscious mind. In fact, experts say that only about 5 percent of the activities we perform are driven by the conscious mind. The other 95 percent are driven by the subconscious mind.

The conscious mind is like the top of an iceberg, visible above the surface of the ocean. The subconscious mind is the enormous bulk beneath the waves. That's where the real power lives. And what's important to understand about the subconscious mind is that it's not just a self-contained personal set of beliefs, habits, and ideas. Our subconscious minds are permeable to those around us and influenced by the cultures and life circumstances we find ourselves in. Most of our parents' fears and neuroses and anxieties are downloaded into our subconscious mind, along with all the problems in the culture around us. And the momentum of all those subconscious habits is a big part of what directs the energy in our lives. But that subconscious mind is also connected to the creative energy of the universe, and we can use it to tap into that divine abundance and love that some people call God.

Think about a pilot flying a 747. Yes, his hand is on the wheel and he's looking out for anything unusual. But most of the functions the plane are running by themselves. We're like that too—we breathe on autopilot, our hearts beat on autopilot, we drive to work on autopilot, we chew and digest our food on autopilot.

All of that makes sense—it would take a tremendous amount of energy if we had to do all of those things consciously. We tend to become conscious of these functions only when something goes wrong. If your heart suddenly starts racing, you become conscious of it pretty quickly, just as the 747 pilot will become conscious of the plane's altitude if it suddenly plummets. But there are a lot of other things we do subconsciously—actions and choices and habits—that define our destiny. Those things are what we need to shine some light on. We need to reprogram our subconscious mind so that it takes us in the direction we actually want to go in, rather than simply following the tracks laid down by our parents and our culture.

"Do not conform any longer to the pattern of this world, but be transformed by the renewing of your mind."

—St. Paul, *Romans 12:2, NIV*

The key to attracting your heart's desires, therefore, is to find a way to reprogram your subconscious mind. It's not enough to just think positive thoughts a few times a day and expect the world to fall at your feet. You need to get "beneath the hood," so to speak, and this requires a deeper level of commitment. Wayne Dyer, one of the great contemporary teachers of the art of manifestation, says, "For me, manifesting is not about attracting what you want. Manifesting is an awareness and an understanding that you attract what you are."[3] In line with this thinking, you have to change the subconscious patterns of your being to reflect abundance and fulfillment if you are going to attract abundance and fulfillment into your life. If your subconscious mind is convinced that you are wounded, deprived, and needy, that is what you will manifest.

This was the essential lesson that John taught me that day. He asked me to tell him my number-one dream, and then he explained that we needed to write it down on a blank sheet of paper in such a way that it felt not like a future hope but like a current reality. John told me that this was because time is not real. I decided to ignore that comment, since I had no idea what he was talking about. He quoted Einstein as having said that, "the distinction between past, present, and future is only a stubbornly persistent illusion."[4] He also told me that my description of my dream had to be emotionally powerful and authentic, in order to break the illusion in my subconscious mind that this was not currently true and to allow the energy that flows through the universe, which he referred to as God, to make it an actual reality.

My overriding desire at that point in my life was to be reconciled with my wife and my daughter. So John helped me to craft the following statement:

> *My wife Lisa and I are happily married. Every single day our love for one another grows deeper and stronger. I feel such great peace and love and I am so grateful for this peace and love. My wife loves and adores me and I love and adore her. Our life and love are beautiful and inspire others. Our daughter, Michelle, thrives in this spirit of love. Both parents love her very much and she returns this love unconditionally. I feel so amazingly blessed. All three of us are so happy.*

Writing this was not an easy task for me, because my current emotional state and the reality of my situation could not have been farther from what these words described. Lisa hated me, rightfully so, and my daughter was growing up without a father in her life. It took about forty-five minutes to get the statement written to John's satisfaction. He then assured me that in the seventh week of our work together, he would teach me a magical technique that would make it impossible for my written word not to become a reality. As you can imagine, I was very skeptical.

At the end of the session, John asked me what dream I would like to work on next week. I was uncertain if I would even return. The hour I had spent with him hadn't made me feel better—in fact, I felt worse, because he'd brought all my pain to the surface, so it felt like a raw wound exposed to the rain and biting wind. As I drove away from the session, my arm out the window holding the door shut, I couldn't help but wonder if I had just wasted $50, more than I would make in tips that night after taking eight hours of abuse from drunken diners.

For some reason, however, I went back. This time I took $50 in cash, as my checking account was nearly overdrawn after paying my monthly child support. John opened the door and greeted me with a very sweet and warm smile, telling me how happy he was that I had decided to return. I sat down, thinking that at least it was a sunny day and my arm was dry this time. "What dream would you like to work on?" he asked me. My mind went quickly to my job and how badly the restaurant was run, how poorly they treated the employees. "I want to own my own business," I blurted out. "Okay, that's great," John replied. "Let's get to work."

By the end of that session, we had crafted the following statement:

> *I own my own business and I love it. I focus on taking care of my customers and employees. I love my customers and employees and in return they love me. My business grows stronger every day, and I am so very grateful. My wife and daughter support me in our business. I love that they can be there with me. It makes me feel so incredibly happy. People from all over the area hear about our business and how special it is; it becomes the talk of the town. It gradually grows more and more successful. It is so great to be able to do what I love. It is a joy. Our family is so supported by our business and the love we receive from our employees and customers. Life is good. God is good.*

In the weeks that followed, I crafted similar statements for my intention to earn $10,000 per month, my intention to be healthy and strong physically, and my intention to own my own home.

When the sixth week came around, I had already gone through all of my significant dreams. But I remembered how, when I was a young boy, I had heard my father's stories of his difficult childhood and had a strong desire to help troubled youth (not realizing, at the time, that I would become one). John helped me to write the following intention:

I take much of my money and free time to help teenagers and young adults who are neglected and struggling with their lives. I love the fact that we have created a place where they can be safe, grow emotionally, mentally, and spiritually. I love the difference that I can make to these young people to make the world a better place.

That was the promise I put out to the universe. Perhaps I didn't fully understand at the time what it meant or how important it was, but it felt good to write it—better than any of the statements I had written about what I wanted for myself.

In the seventh and final session, John got out a cassette player and a cassette recorder. He began playing hypnotic music and handed me a script for a relaxation technique. I read the relaxation script, followed by my six intentions, and they were recorded with the music in the background. John told me that I should listen to that cassette tape every morning and night.

Sounds crazy, right? But what's crazier is that it worked. Not overnight but in time, each of the dreams we carefully crafted in our weekly sessions came true. Three years after my first session, out of the blue, my then ex-wife Lisa, who had disliked me passionately since I had abandoned her and our child, called me and asked me to escort her to a Christmas party. We were remarried six months later and had three more children together. Six months after my sessions with John, I put an ad in the paper looking for investors to help me start my own restaurant. Despite having no cash, no credit, and a negative net worth, I was able to raise enough money to open my own business within a year of setting that intention. I have owned my own business almost ever since. My income, which had been less than $2,000 a month when I started seeing John, rose steadily, surpassing my $10,000 a month goal and reaching as high as $300,000 a month at times. I also enjoyed great health despite my earlier abuse of my body with drink and drugs. Soon after my wife and I remarried, we were able to buy a beautiful home with no down payment, and I have since owned even more palatial residences. The only one of my six intentions that did not fully manifest was the last. Although I once taught a course at a juvenile hall, made time to coach little league baseball, and gave the occasional speech at my local church, I did not make good on my promise.

"Underneath your outer form, you are connected with something so vast, so immeasurable and sacred, that it cannot be conceived or spoken of—yet I am speaking of it now. I am speaking of it not to give you something to believe in but to show you how you can know it yourself."

And so I found myself, twenty years after I showed up wet, miserable, and desperate on John's doorstep, standing on the sunlit deck outside my beautiful home, healthy, wealthy, with my beautiful family, yet knowing that something was missing. This

—Eckhart Tolle,
The Power of Now

was the second turning point in my life. The first had been when I had nothing. The second came when I had everything. I didn't change overnight—my path has never been that simple. But it was shortly after this moment of reckoning that I met a beautiful woman named Margot, whose life, and death, would eventually teach me what it meant to fulfill the promise I had made.

Everything's Perfect ... But Something Is Missing

N o matter who you are or where you have come from, you can change your life. But first you have to change your thoughts. And in order to change your thoughts, you have to know what it is you want. This is, in fact, the biggest challenge— knowing what you want. Back when I met the mystery man, I was lucky. I had a very clear picture of what I wanted. Once you have that clear picture of the outcome, it's easy to come up with a plan to get there, and once you have a solid plan the universe will assist you in fulfilling your desire.

"The good news is that the moment you decide that what you know is more important than what you have been taught to believe, you will have shifted gears in your quest for abundance. Success comes from within, not from without."

—Richard Carlson, *Don't Sweat the Small Stuff About Money*

Part of the problem is that we've all been programmed with society's definitions of success. We're running on what social scientists call the "hedonic treadmill"—the endless pursuit of material things that we've been told will bring us happiness. Sometimes we end up living out our parents' definitions of success. We become a doctor or a lawyer because that's what success meant to them and they never had the chance to make it. We feel obligated to fulfill their dreams because they gave us the opportunities they never had in order for us to do so.

Our definitions of success also change over time. For me, for a long time, success just meant having money. But when I made such a mess of my early life, I reached a point where success meant being free of my addictions—smoking, gambling, drinking, drugs. Later, success came to mean getting my wife and daughter back, or creating a stable life for our family.

For some people, the definition of success is to "be happy." But that's an elusive goal, as most of us discover. I used to think that money would make me happy, but I found out, as most people who become rich tend to do, that money does not equal happiness. That's not a new revelation, by any means. These days there are countless books, academic studies, and popular articles dedicated to the subject. Thanks to the field of research known as the "science of happiness," we not only know that money won't make us happy (at least not once we get above $75,000 a year), but we can find cultural, psychological, physical, economic, and evolutionary reasons to help explain why. I'm not against making a lot of money—as Woody Allen says, it's "better than poverty, if only for financial reasons." [5] And it can become a tool for doing tremendous good, which is much more likely to make you happy than simply being rich.

One of the problems with the pursuit of happiness as a definition of success is that it tends to make us live in the future, dissatisfied with the present moment. Daniel Gilbert writes in *Stumbling on Happiness* that, "We treat our future selves as though they were our children, spending most of the hours of most of our days constructing tomorrows that we hope will make them happy . . . squirreling away portions of our paychecks each month so that *they* can enjoy their retirements on a putting green, jogging and flossing with some regularity so that *they* can avoid coronaries and gum grafts." [6] Unfortunately, we're usually not too good at predicting what will make our future selves happy, often overestimating the impact of getting certain things we think that we want. How many times have you pinned your hopes of happiness on getting that new car, or new house, only to end up disappointed? Gilbert concludes that it is a well-intentioned but unfulfilling way to live, performing daily "acts of charity" for our future selves who, "like the fruits of our loins . . . are often thankless." [7]

Too much focus on future happiness not only leads to dissatisfaction, but it can also create a miserable life in the present. As the great Buddhist teacher Thich Nhat Hanh writes, "Our notions about happiness entrap us. We forget that they are just ideas. Our idea of happiness can prevent us from actually being happy. We fail to see the opportunity for joy that is right in front of us when we are caught in a belief that happiness should take a particular form." [8] Rather than focus on happiness as a goal with a particular form, I'd suggest that you see it as a byproduct of activities that have purpose and meaning. Pursue your purpose and you'll be surprised by how happy it makes you in the present moment. This is a hard lesson to learn for most Americans, however, who have grown up thinking of "the pursuit of happiness" as our constitutional birthright. Interestingly, as Marci Shimoff points out in *Happy for No Reason,* the word "pursuit" in Jefferson's day actually did not mean to "chase after" something; it meant to "practice" it. [9] Practicing happiness is a very different idea than chasing after it. I've found that the best way to practice happiness is to know that I am living up to my fullest capacity to do good in the world.

I have come to believe that, in the broadest sense, this is what we are all here for. We are designed to give. We may not all be fortunate enough to have excess money to give away, but we can all give of *ourselves*—of our energy, our creativity, our strengths, our unique capacities. When we find a way to satisfy our own deepest desires and serve others at the same time, we will be living a fulfilling life. Don't think of giving as something you will do someday after you've gotten everything you need for yourself—that's the mistake I made. And that "someday" didn't come until I had suffered through the painful realization that all the "stuff"

"I don't know what your destiny will be, but one thing I do know: the only ones among you who will be really happy are those who have sought and found how to serve."

—Albert Schweitzer, addressing a group of students in 1950

I'd accumulated didn't make me happy. Giving should not be an afterthought—it should be woven into every step of your journey, because it is the missing piece that will bring you happiness and amplify the love in the universe. And paradoxically, it is your generosity of spirit that will also allow you to enjoy all the fruits of your success in the present moment. Numerous recent studies confirm the connection between doing good and feeling good. As researcher Stephen G. Post, Ph.D., notes in a 2011 review of the field: "A strong correlation exists between the well-being, happiness, health, and longevity of people who are emotionally kind and compassionate."[10] Rosabeth Moss Kanter of Harvard Business School observes that, "The happiest people I know are dedicated to dealing with the most difficult problems."[11]

Redefining Success

So what does success mean for you? Arianna Huffington, founder of the *Huffington Post*, told the Smith College class of 2013 in her commencement address that, "At the moment, our society's notion of success is largely composed of two parts: money and power." However, she said, "Money and power by themselves are a two-legged stool—you can balance on them for a while, but eventually you're going to topple over." "What we need is a more humane and sustainable definition of success," she argued, that includes "well-being, wisdom, our ability to wonder, and to give back."[12]

I wholeheartedly agree with that sentiment. I wish someone had told me that when I was the age of those graduates. Another perspective on success that I like is one that a friend shared with me a long time ago. He had seen it stuck on the refrigerator door at a friend's house and it stuck in his mind: "There are many ways to define success, but one of the best ways to measure success is how your children speak about you when you're not around." I have no idea who wrote it, but that quote inspired me to live a life that my kids would be proud of.

It's important to take the time to really consider what success means for you, because it will help you make the important decisions in life, knowing that you have a clear goal. I made some of my biggest life choices without even a thought—including the decision to get married, which I made while drinking, and the decision to have children, which just kind of happened. And while I don't regret any of those things, I have come to believe that it is far better to think clearly and deeply about what we want in life, and make these decisions consciously, taking full responsibility for the consequences. Otherwise we are likely to make others suffer and to suffer ourselves, as I did.

Sometimes suffering is an inevitable part of the journey. We can't avoid all mistakes or wrong turns. But I believe we can avoid some of the unnecessary kinds of suffering by just giving a little more thought to our choices and our direction in life. And if we want to make a significant impact in the world or in the lives of other people, it gets even more important that we think clearly about where we are going. Living a life with a higher purpose requires a direct and pointed map system for the universe to follow.

I say "the universe," because remember, you are not going about this alone. You are inviting in the abundance of the universe, and in order for that to work, you have to direct your thoughts, both conscious and subconscious, toward the goal you have defined. In *Beyond Success,* author Jeffrey Gitterman compares the subconscious to a navigation system. "We're constantly being given directions by our subconscious mind," he writes, "but if we haven't plugged in the right address with our conscious mind, then our subconscious mind is going to lead us round in circles."[13] When you get crystal clear about your goals and dreams, you give the universal energy clear directions about where to take you and what to bring you.

No one else can create or define what your life's desires are, so you must be willing to question yourself rigorously and deeply. Sit down with a pen and paper and make a list of the highest priorities in your life, including this element of compassion and service to others. Once again, including that piece does not mean you should hesitate to seek wealth and abundance for yourself as well. But it will all be amplified if you allow it to flow freely to you and through you, then out into the world. As the comedian Louis C.K. says, "I never viewed money as being 'my money.' I always saw it as 'The Money.' It's a resource. If it pools up around me, then it needs to be flushed back out into the system."[14]

Sometimes, especially if we've had a hard life lacking in love or money or success, it can be natural to want to guard our achievements and our gains, to hold them close for fear of losing them. We are afraid that giving to others will decrease our own wealth or energy or love.

Deeply, we're convinced that there is not enough to go around. In fact, that's not how the universe works. When we give, we amplify all of these things. Generous people attract more of the energy of the universe so that their giving leaves them feeling fuller and often leads to greater material success as well.

The purpose of this chapter is for you to break out of those limiting fears and beliefs so you can magnify your dreams—bring them into focus and enlarge their power and impact. I'm going to share with you two exercises that I call Dream Magnifiers, which together will help you to achieve this clarity and focus. Each of these exercises will remove some of the limiting beliefs that act like blinders, obscuring the enormous potential our lives can have. Let's dream big!

Dream Magnifier #1: One Week to Live

If you want to find out what's really important to you, ask yourself the following question:

What you would do if you had only one week to live?

Think about it seriously and really try to imagine yourself in that position. Who would you spend your time with? Would you waste time on petty arguments, road rage, or gossip? Would this be a time to exact revenge on all those who wronged you or a time to let it all go and forgive? Who would you show extra love or kindness to? How would you communicate that to them? Imagine exactly what you would say. Write it down.

Would you show yourself extra love as well? Perhaps you would forgive yourself for past mistakes and wrong decisions. Maybe this would be the moment to fully accept yourself—your flaws, your strengths, your beauty, your weaknesses—and realize that you are enough. You have given it your best shot with the tools you have been given and the opportunities that presented themselves, and even if you haven't, that's okay too. Forgiveness is a beautiful thing when extended to yourself or to other people. It gives you freedom to love unconditionally. Write down the things you would forgive yourself for.

How would you live that last week? What values would guide your choices? When presented with the immediacy of death, it becomes harder to hold on to negative feelings like jealousy, hate, and anger. Maybe that's simply because you have one week left to live and you would rather spend it doing things that make you happy. But what you may also be realizing is that these intense negative emotions take up a lot of energy. They are contradictory to the universal energy that swirls within us all as loving, empathetic beings. If you had only a week to live, wouldn't you want to prioritize the most important things in life—the things that bring love and joy to you and those around you? Anger, hate, and jealousy are all excess baggage, and the sooner you drop these bags the sooner you become free to accept the abundance of love. Think about what you would let go of if you had only a week to live, and what would be the values and actions you would prioritize. Write them down.

The results of this exercise will reveal what your deeper priorities are by removing the overshadowing distractions that tend to manifest when you think you have plenty of time. At first, this **exercise** may seem like the opposite of what I promised—I had said I would remove limitations, and here I am giving you a deadline! But in fact, the deadline is liberating. It frees you from the distractions and less important things that might cloud your attention. The illusion that we have all the time in the world is, paradoxically, a limitation on our ability to see clearly and directly what matters most to us. As you will hear from many people who have been given the news that they only have a limited time to live, that literal "deadline" gives you the freedom to drop all other distractions in life and prioritize the people and values you hold most dear.

"Make no little plans. They have no magic to stir men's blood."

—Daniel Burnham

Dream Magnifier #2: Financial Freedom

Here's a second question to help you clarify your life's purpose:

If you had a guarantee that you would live a long and healthy life and money was not a factor, what mission would you embark upon?

Many of us find it hard to envision a life free from the worries of debt, bills, and health issues. These anxieties make it difficult for us to think beyond our own day-to-day survival and welfare, let alone think about helping others. Sometimes we don't even see the good we could do in the world because our vision is obscured by our survival needs. This exercise can help you to see beyond those limitations so that you can create a vision. It may not take away the immediate need to deal with your own circumstances, but you may find that you are able to do so with much more purpose and energy if you are guided by a higher vision of what it will make possible.

It's true that the basic needs in life do have to be taken care of in order to free our energy and attention for a higher purpose. Psychologist Abraham Maslow showed this in his Hierarchy of Needs, which is a very useful model to help us understand ourselves. He represented human needs as a pyramid, with our most primal survival needs at the base, followed by safety needs; the need for love, affection, and belonging; the need for self-esteem; and, finally, the need for self-actualization. Late in his life, he added one more level at the peak of the pyramid: the need for self-transcendence. The great insight of Maslow's model was his assertion that the lower-level "deficiency" needs generally must be fulfilled before the individual can become concerned about some of the higher-level "being" needs. "A hungry man may willingly surrender his need for self-respect in order to stay alive," he wrote, "but once he can feed, shelter, and clothe himself, he becomes likely to seek higher needs."[15]

That being said, let's imagine that you've ascended Maslow's pyramid and have not only satisfied your survival needs but are fulfilled in your self-esteem and need for love. What would you do then? Imagine your potential with perfect health and financial freedom! Many of us limit our dreams to what seems reasonable or rationally attainable. When we dream small dreams we receive small realities. By allowing yourself to release the fear of financial insecurity or physical impediments, you can dream infinitely. Remember when your parents and teachers told you that you could be anything that you wanted to be? That you could change the world if you believed in yourself? That's the spirit this exercise is designed to activate in you. Forget everything you were told once you grew older and all of those same people began giving you more limited and "practical" advice when you shared with them your idealistic and grandiose dreams. Forget the cynics who told you to "get real." Give yourself permission to amplify your wildest dreams and *make* them real!

So what mission would you pursue if you were assured perfect health and financial freedom? You don't need to figure out how to make money from this dream or how you will raise funds to complete it. Do you feel how that shifts your attention? Your dreams just opened up. You could dream of your intense passion for climbing mountains, your desire to feed the hungry in the refugee camps of Kenya, or your love for healthy eating and sharing that knowledge with others. You might find that something you have only considered to be a hobby—your passion for music or your time spent volunteering with disadvantaged youth—is actually the thing you want to give all of your time and attention to. If you remove the "but" that comes with financial concerns, you will begin to see more clearly what you really care about.

Write down the answer to this question, and then compare it with the answers to the previous question. Between those two you will find the sweet spot of your life's purpose. Free your dreams from the external conditions related to time, money, and health, and see what limitless possibilities arise. Whatever matters most to you when you are free from the belief that you have all the time in the world, free of the limitations that come from thinking you don't have enough money—that is your dream. Imagine it. Envision it. What would your day look like if you were living this dream? What would the quality of your life look like? What happiness would it generate for you and for others in your life? How would it impact people around you?

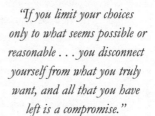

"If you limit your choices only to what seems possible or reasonable . . . you disconnect yourself from what you truly want, and all that you have left is a compromise."

—Robert Fritz,
The Path of Least Resistance

How to Manifest Your Dreams

Now that you have magnified your dreams, I am going to teach you the manifestation process that I was taught by the mystery man more than three decades ago. What I've added to the process is the lesson I learned: that *love is a promise that must be kept.* I'm giving you the opportunity to include the all-important element of giving in to your dreams from the beginning, rather than have to go through the disillusionment I had to go through before adding that critical piece. Here is the five-step process:

Manifestation Process

1. Clearly identify your life's true desires, with love and compassion as an underlying element throughout.
2. Write down your desires as a present reality, in positive terms, making them emotionally convincing—connect as much positive emotion to them as you can.
3. Choose some background music. (Search for "theta brainwave music.")
4. Set up a recording device, play the background music, and read the relaxation script (below), followed by your written desires.
5. Listen to your recording daily, as often as possible—at a minimum, every morning and night.

Let's walk through those steps one by one.

1. Clearly identify your life's true desires, with love and compassion as an underlying element throughout. This is what the Dream Magnifier exercises we've just done are designed to help you with. If you can focus on what you would do if you had only one week to live and then on what you would do if you had complete financial freedom and perfect health, then the combination of these two things is the sweet spot for your dreams. There may be several desires that you want to work on, which represent steps toward your definition of success. For example, if your purpose in life is to help solve the problem of climate change, you might first set a desire that relates to becoming wealthy and self-sufficient so that your time and energy and resources will be free to dedicate to that life purpose. Although I believe that all things are possible, you need to start with intentions that are within reason. Why? Because you have been conditioned to believe in limitations. As you recondition your belief system to accept that all things are possible, you can increase your dreams, goals, and desires as you progress.

2. Write down your desires as a present reality, in positive terms, making them emotionally convincing—connect as much positive emotion to them as you can.

It's important to follow these specific instructions. As I explained in the previous chapter, this process works on the principle that time is an illusion. So you need to break that illusion by asserting that your desires are already true. The second instruction is also critical: the universe does not understand "negative" language. Here are some examples:

Negative language	Positive language
"I have no debt."	"I have an abundance of money"
"My partner and I do not fight."	"I have a loving and caring relationship with my partner."
"My work is no longer tedious."	"I have a fulfilling and impactful career."

As further examples, I'll share with you two of my current dream statements, related to my desire to serve (through my Love From Margot Foundation) and my desire for love. You'll see that these are written in the present tense and in positive language, and I've also tried to make them as emotionally rich and convincing as possible:

> *I am raising millions of dollars through the Love From Margot Foundation. This money is used to help those in financial need who are fighting a serious or terminal illness. The money flows in so quickly, beyond my wildest expectations. I am blessed, and thousands are being blessed through this Foundation. Thank you.*

> *I have amazing love in my life. I am so truly blessed—so many people truly love me, and their love lifts me up so that I may serve as many as possible. I love all people at a heart and soul level. I understand that not everyone is awake, so I love their potential to awaken.*

3. Choose some background music. Instrumental music is best for this, and ideally it should be something that you find soothing and relaxing. Try searching YouTube for "theta brainwave music."

4. Set up a recording device, play the background music, and read the relaxation script followed by your written desires. You'll find the relaxation script on the following page. Read it slowly and clearly, keeping your tone of voice even and calm and pausing between phrases. These days, you don't have to use two cassette players like John did for me. You can use your computer, your iPad, or your smartphone. When you read your written desires, read them with as much emotional conviction as you can muster. The power lies in the fact that your desires are recorded in your own voice, with positive feelings attached.

5. Listen to your recording daily, and as often as possible—at a minimum, both morning and night. The best time to do this, I have found, is right when you wake up and just before you fall asleep. When your mind is in that twilight zone between sleeping and waking, you have more access to your subconscious, before your conscious mind has fully come online. As you are listening to the recording of the relaxation script, close your eyes and allow each part of your body to relax as the script describes.

"See the things that you want as already yours. Know that they will come to you at need. Then let them come. Don't fret and worry about them. Don't think about your lack of them. Think of them as yours, as belonging to you, as already in your possession."

—Robert Collier,
Secret of the Ages

Relaxation Script

My breathing is slow and easy and relaxed. I inhale deeply and exhale slowly and gently. Again I breathe . . . and again . . . I am so relaxed and peaceful.

I am grateful for this special moment. I am grateful for everything.

I am relaxed, my breathing is relaxed, and as I gently breathe in and out, I am at peace and my mind is quiet. I am relaxed.

The muscles in my face are relaxed, my jaw muscles are relaxed. I bite down on my teeth and then release; my face and jaw are relaxed.

My neck is relaxed. I turn my neck in a circle a few times, and my neck is relaxed.

My shoulders are relaxed. I pull back and shrug my shoulders; my shoulders are relaxed.

I am so very relaxed; my breathing is so gentle, natural, and relaxed.

My arms are relaxed. Hanging gently from my shoulders, my arms are relaxed.

My hands are relaxed. I squeeze my hands into a fist tightly and then release the grip; my hands are relaxed.

I am relaxed, I breathe gently in and out and I love the sensation. I am grateful for the gift of breath.

My stomach muscles are relaxed. I tighten them and then release them; my stomach is relaxed. My butt muscles are relaxed. I tighten them and release them; my buttocks are relaxed. I am relaxed.

My hamstrings are relaxed. I tighten them and then release them; my hamstrings are relaxed. I am relaxed.

My hips are relaxed. My blood flows through my hip joints, healing my joints and bringing me peace. My hips are open and relaxed.

My thighs are relaxed. I am relaxed.

My knees work perfectly, my knees are relaxed, my knees serve me.

I am relaxed, my breath is relaxed, I am at peace.

I am so very grateful, I love myself and everything in my life. I am love, I am relaxed.

My calves are relaxed. I stretch my calves and my calves are relaxed.

My ankles are relaxed. I move my ankles in a circle and my ankles are relaxed; I am relaxed.

I am at deep peace, I am relaxed.

My feet are relaxed. My feet ground me to Mother Earth, and my feet are very relaxed. I wiggle my toes; my toes are relaxed.

I am relaxed and in a deep and grateful space, one with all, one with the energy of the universe.

I am all-powerful, I am love, I am peace, I am free to create my heart's desire.

I am relaxed.

I am.

The last piece of advice I will give you is that you need to be committed and be patient. In our culture, we're hooked on instant gratification. We've become accustomed to wanting everything now and giving up when we don't get it right away. The universe doesn't work that way, just as God didn't show up on the steps of the church that day when I hit rock bottom and demanded he do so. In retrospect, the energy and power that I have come to understand as the equivalent of God showed up in every specific form that I asked for. It took some time, and it took some discipline on my part, but the results exceeded even the most audacious dreams that I could have come up with. Magnify your dreams, put them out into the universe with commitment and patience, then sit back and watch in wonder as the power of love comes into your life.

Love is Stronger Than Fear

Can you remember a time when you had no fear? A time before life taught you to protect yourself? Growing up with my father's drinking problem and unpredictable temper, I could hardly remember what it felt like not to be instinctively defensive. It was only much later in life, as my heart started to open and I learned to trust, that memories surfaced—memories of a time in early childhood when I had an innate sense that all beings were connected and that life was love. Somewhere before the fear set in, before I hardened myself against my father's anger and constant humiliations, was a faraway oasis of peace and joy and fearlessness.

> *"Love is what we were born with. Fear is what we learned here."*
> —Marianne Williamson,
> *A Return to Love*

My circumstances were genuinely frightening for a child, so it's no surprise that I lost touch with that undefensive state. But even those who grow up in more loving, supportive environments seem to get the message sooner or later from the culture around us: life is not safe. We all come into this world as innocent little beings of energy and love. But at some point, our parents reject us or get angry at us, or we pick up the emotion of situations around us. We begin downloading information from our parents, our teachers, our environment, the media, and the society we live in. We learn how we must behave in order to be accepted, what we should believe and what we should not believe, who we should trust and who we should not trust. We start erecting barriers around our hearts, barriers that divide us and cement the differences between us.

These barriers serve a purpose. They protect us from getting hurt too badly, by life and by other people. But the protection comes at a price. The walls around our hearts keep out more than just the pain—they can also keep love out and hold us back from giving love. Fear is perhaps the greatest filter to our ability to love— fear that has been programmed into us since childhood; fear that arises from our past wounds and betrayals; fear that we are inadequate or incapable or unworthy. If love is the essential force in the universe, fear is the counterforce. Free yourself from fear and you will be amazed by the power of love that is released within you.

Freeing yourself from fear does not mean that the feeling of fear has to go away. It means you choose to no longer allow fear to rule your choices and actions. Unless you make this choice, the underlying fear can create significant obstacles in your relationships, in your career, in your spiritual growth. I even speak about this with my salespeople at the car dealership, because I've discovered that the number-one obstacle to successful selling is the salesperson's fear of rejection. As a result of their own woundedness, they're not willing to put themselves out there fully and really connect with customers. When they let go of this fear of rejection, I've seen people's success rates suddenly double. The same principle applies in relationships. If you're in a powerful love relationship but you're uncomfortable with your own being, that fear will creep in—the fear of rejection or loss. And it will prevent you from giving yourself fully to that other person.

Fear limits what's possible. Once we are able to drop the fear we have been programmed into believing and the defense systems we have constructed to protect ourselves, we can begin to unlock the magic that flows from realizing that we are all connected by the energy of love.

If you've been blessed with an easier journey in life or you've done a lot of spiritual growth or personal development work, your defenses may not be so difficult to let down. But for many of us, it is a greater challenge. Our life experiences, too often, have served to reinforce those barriers. The wounds of a difficult childhood, an abusive relationship, a betrayal, or a loss can turn into a kind of scar tissue around the heart, thick and numb, shielding us from future pain. When these scars grow hard, it can be difficult to ever truly love another or allow oneself to be loved. Although the scars may not show on the surface, they condemn us to a fearful and lonely existence, isolated inside ourselves. That was how I lived: holding up the façade of a successful life but inwardly feeling hollow and desperate. But thanks to my beautiful wife Margot, even someone as wounded as I was had the opportunity to learn the second great lesson of my life: that *love is stronger than fear.* In order to share with you how I learned this, I will need to briefly tell our story.

Left-field Love

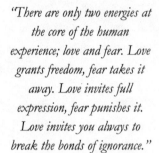

The day I met Margot is still etched in my mind as vividly as if it were yesterday. It was not long after that day when I had stood on my deck and admitted to myself, for the first time, that even though everything in my life was perfect, I was not happy.

"There are only two energies at the core of the human experience; love and fear. Love grants freedom, fear takes it away. Love invites full expression, fear punishes it. Love invites you always to break the bonds of ignorance."

—Neale Donald Walsh, *Communion with God*

That feeling of hollowness was still with me as I drove to work on the morning of November 17, 2000. I'd pulled my Porsche out of the driveway of my beautiful home, driven past the manicured lawns and elegant mansions of my neighborhood with that same question gnawing at me: *What are you doing with your life?* Once again, I pushed the thought away—it seemed like such a selfish and ungrateful question to be asking myself, especially since the universe had given me everything I had ever asked for. I was too proud to admit, even to myself, that my "perfect life" was not so perfect. I'd worked so hard to become the successful businessman, the good husband, the beloved father. And I was afraid. I had overcome addiction, debt, divorce, and self-hatred. But the fear that had gripped me when I had nothing had not been appeased by getting everything. It was not so close to the surface anymore, but it ran deeper—I was terrified of the emptiness that all my wealth and status had brought me and the feeling that there was no way out of the gilded cage I had created for myself.

I probably would have never fully admitted how I felt, much less found the courage to leave it all behind, if the promise of extraordinary love had not walked into my office that day in the form of a beautiful advertising sales rep named Margot. The moment our eyes met there was an intensity between us that floored me. Yes, she was beautiful—a twenty-seven-year-old Peruvian woman with glowing golden skin, glossy dark hair, and alluring brown eyes. But what captivated me was something more than physical attraction. I almost felt as if I already knew her intimately and was just recognizing her familiar face after a long separation. Carl Jung once wrote that "the meeting of two personalities is like the contact of two chemical substances: if there is any reaction, both are transformed." [16] That's how it was with Margot. There was an immediate, mysterious chemistry between us that would end up truly transforming us both.

Let me just say right here that I am not proud of the way our relationship began and I would never advise anyone to take the road of infidelity, as we did. But I must be honest about what happened, and I hope my readers will not jump too quickly to judge me or our relationship. In the months following that first meeting, Margot and I began to work together, and unbeknownst to each other, we were both falling in love. I couldn't explain it, but I felt a deep sense of recognition when I was with her—as if I'd already known her for lifetimes. I instinctively trusted her, which surprised me—I didn't trust anyone. Eventually, after many months, we could no longer deny what we were feeling, and we crossed the line from friends and colleagues to lovers.

If there's any lesson I learned from this period of my life, it's that honesty is absolutely essential. To this day, one of my greatest regrets is that Margot and I began our love with subterfuge, neither of us initially having the clarity or courage to tell the truth to our spouses and deal with the consequences. Eventually the truth came out, as it always does, and we all suffered through the pain of our choices. But while I wish we had gone about it differently, I can never regret our coming together. Something deeper was connecting us, something that neither of us could explain but both of us felt undeniably. As Steve Jobs told the graduates at Stanford University in his commencement speech, "You can't connect the dots looking forward; you can only connect them looking backwards." Looking back now, I can see the beauty of our love and the rightness of it, despite the unnecessary pain caused by our all-too-human weaknesses and poor choices. And I can see how everything worked out for the best—how my first wife Lisa found new love and happiness, how Margot's husband remarried and had the children she could not have given him, and how Margot's love made me the person I am today, a person I could never have become without her. But none of this is an excuse for my poor judgment at the time or lessens my regret over my dishonesty.

As Nietzsche said, there is always some madness in love, but in our case there was powerful sanity too. When it was just me and her together, everything seemed to make sense in a way that nothing else in our lives did at the time. With her, I felt like the best version of myself. She brought out my potential, allowing me to be the person I had always wanted to be, but had been too afraid, too self-critical, too wounded to be. She had a way of loving me—the real me—not the image of Mike Murphy that I had worked hard to create: successful businessman, father, and husband. She loved my essence, the child in me who knew there was a deeper meaning to life.

That's not to say our love was perfect. She was a hot-tempered Latina, and I was an Irishman with a taste for drink—we had more than our share of fights. But she never seemed to hold a grudge or blame me for my shortcomings. Margot's way of loving me sometimes infuriated me. I felt like I had nowhere to run and nowhere to hide. She realized my potential to love and would go to any lengths to help me fulfill it. At some point during the first few months of our relationship, she wrote to me: "I hope one day to love you with no walls. I will wait forever if you ask me to."

Early on, I realized that Margot had an unusual capacity to love and be loved. I remember one time, early in our romance, when we were having dinner at a Mexican restaurant in San Jose. Her phone just kept ringing, and she took every call, giving each friend her undivided attention. After about the tenth call, I joked that one day I would write a sitcom called "Everybody Loves Margot." Because it was true. And she loved them back, with an unreserved trust and open heart that I'd never encountered before. She had a rare ability to see the good in people and to recognize the love in their hearts even when they were displaying their worst sides. When she began to love me, I didn't know how to receive that kind of love. She saw through to the good in my heart even when my woundedness left me reluctant to trust or commit. She believed in me even through years when my painful indecision and unreliability drove her crazy.

Thanks to Margot's example, I have learned that the greatest gift you can give another is to see beyond their anger or aggression to their fear, and to see beyond their fear to their true essence, which is love. If you can believe in another person like this, even when everything they do is communicating the opposite, you give them the precious opportunity to become that best part of who they are.

Margot never stopped holding out that opportunity to me. She loved me no matter what I did. Somewhere, I knew this, despite my instinctive mistrust and my continual attempts at self-sabotage. I knew she'd always be there for me. And somehow she knew that I'd always be there for her, although to this day I don't know how she saw it despite all evidence to the contrary. "I know that you are strong and you will protect me," she wrote in one email. "I know that, and that's why I love you so much." It took many years for me to begin to truly appreciate the gift of love I'd been given. I was tied up in guilt and self-hatred for what I'd done to my previous wife, for the pain I'd caused my children and the way that I'd jeopardized my hard-earned financial success in divorce court. Margot's patience, and the steadiness of her love while I found my way, was a miracle for which I am eternally grateful.

Embracing the Shadow

As I later learned, I was struggling with what pioneering psychotherapist Carl Jung, as well as contemporary psychologists and spiritual teachers, call "the shadow." The shadow is commonly defined as those

"You may be hurt if you love too much, but you will live in misery if you love too little."
— Napoleon Hill,
Napoleon Hill's Positive Action Plan

aspects of ourselves that we don't want to see—the things we have pushed outside of our conscious experience of self. Childhood wounds, fear, anger, shame, guilt—all of these are common aspects of the shadow for many of us. They're the things that are too uncomfortable to bring into the light of consciousness, things that we are afraid of admitting to ourselves and even more afraid of revealing to others. We store these things away deep down inside, and go about our lives as though they didn't exist. Typically, the shadow contains mostly negative aspects of self, but for some people, particularly those with low self-esteem, the shadow can also contain positive aspects of self that for some reason they are reluctant to embrace.

As I've explained, we learn very early in childhood to mistrust life and other people. We also learn to fear our own shadows. When a thought or feeling arises that makes us uncomfortable or we react in a way that we think is unacceptable, we run away from it, shielding ourselves from ourselves. Unfortunately, we can no more run away from our own shadow than I could escape my childhood demons by catching a bus to

Lexington, Kentucky. As Debbie Ford points out in *The Shadow Effect*, "although ignoring or repressing our dark side is the norm, the sobering truth is that running from the shadow only intensifies its power. Denying it only leads to more pain, suffering, regret, and resignation." She calls this "the shadow effect"—the psychological mechanism that kicks in when we fail to take responsibility for integrating our own shadows. The shadow then takes control of us rather than us taking control of the shadow. "Our dark side then starts making our decisions for us, stripping us of our right to make conscious choices, whether it's what food we will eat, how much money we will spend, or what addiction we will succumb to. Our shadow incites us to act out in ways we never imagined we could and to waste our vital energy on bad habits and repetitive behaviors. Our shadow keeps us from full self-expression, from speaking our truth, and from living an authentic life." [17] Looking back, I was a textbook case.

Another common expression of shadow is that we project the aspects of ourselves that we don't want to see onto others around us. For example, I was terrified of my own unreliability and volatility—the cowardice that would drive me to pack up and run at a moment's notice. But because I was unwilling to embrace that aspect of myself and be vulnerable all over again to the woundedness that had caused it, I often projected it onto others—mistrusting their commitment and loyalty. I did this to Margot far too often in the early days of our relationship—trying to curb her fun-loving spirit and independent lifestyle. The result was simply that I pushed her away with my mistrust and my desire to control her.

Embracing our own shadows is a critical step in letting love in. If we cannot compassionately accept all aspects of ourselves, we will always find it hard to fully open our hearts to other people. When we do embrace our shadows, the effect can be surprising and uplifting. As Ford points out, it is often the opposite of what we fear we will experience. "Instead of shame, we feel compassion. Instead of embarrassment, we gain courage. Instead of limitation, we experience freedom. . . . The compassion we discover for ourselves will ignite confidence and courage as we open our hearts to those around us. The power we unearth will help us tackle the fear that has been holding us back and will urge us to move powerfully toward our highest potential. Far from frightening, embracing the shadow allows us to be whole, to be real, to take back our power, to unleash our passion, and to realize our dreams."[18]

When you realize that by avoiding the parts of yourself that you are afraid of, you actually empower them, it can give you the courage to start making space in consciousness for your shadow. There are many great teachers out there who have developed processes for befriending the shadow. The first step is usually to start looking for clues as to where it is hiding.

"When we show only our bright side to the world, our shadow grows restless, sucking into itself much of our energy and passion."

—Elizabeth Lesser, *Broken Open*

Pay attention to your reactivity, to the things you are afraid of or ashamed of revealing and the things you tend to project onto others. These things can point you toward the form your particular shadow takes. Once you identify these clues, Robert Augustus Masters, an expert psycho-spiritual guide, offers some helpful advice on dealing with your own shadow: "The optimal strategy for handling our shadow is to develop *intimacy* with it—this means getting close enough to it to see and feel it in detail, but not so close that we lose the capacity to keep it in focus." And he advises: "As you cultivate intimacy with your shadow, you will inevitably find yourself in various situations which activate your shadow, but you will be far more likely now to work more skillfully with this: You might get into a charged disagreement with your partner, you may have an upsetting encounter with a coworker, you may flare up in reactivity, you may be triggered by a disappointment—but whatever happens, you'll be much more able to take it as an opportunity to see your shadow more clearly, and to make wiser use of it.[19]

Go slowly with this process, and don't be too hard on yourself if you find it challenging to bring your shadow to light. A lifetime of avoidance will not be turned around in a single day. But if you sincerely want to stop being unconsciously driven by the shadow aspects of yourself, you will find the courage to gently but persistently expand the field of your conscious awareness to include the things you fear the most. You will discover the joy of wholeness, of being an integrated human being who is not intimidated by the best or the worst of yourself.

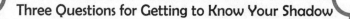

Three Questions for Getting to Know Your Shadow

By its nature, our shadow is a part of us that we have difficulty seeing. We've spent a lifetime burying these aspects of ourselves, so they don't generally come to light overnight. As you begin the journey of embracing your shadow, here are some questions that might help you to identify the parts of yourself that you've habitually kept hidden.

1. What kinds of situations do I tend to overreact to? These might provide clues to the types of childhood wounds or traumas that need to be healed. Follow the trail gently back into your subconscious. What feelings come up in those situations? What memories do those feelings trigger?

2. What am I most afraid that people might find out about me? Let yourself see, in the privacy of your own mind, the things that you are most ashamed of. What are you afraid would happen if someone else could see those parts of yourself? Would it really be so bad? The parts of yourself that you try hardest to hide are often the ones that end up unconsciously driving you.

3. What motives or emotions do I tend to project onto others? When you're afraid of certain aspects of yourself, it's a common psychological habit to start imagining that you see those qualities in others around you and then react to those projections. Next time you feel that happening, stop and ask yourself if it is really him or her or if it is the projection of your own unconscious emotional states.

73

Love Trumps Fear

Margot's battle with cancer began only ten months after we got together. I found a lump in her breast, which, when she

"Too many of us are not living our dreams because we are living our fears."
—Les Brown

finally got it checked out, turned out to be malignant. So began a nine-year journey of chemo, surgeries, tests, results, remission, and recurrence. In the early days of her illness, in the midst of it all, I was struggling with my own demons. Paralyzed by fear, unable to fully commit, I almost drove her away with my indecision. Finally, in 2006, I found the courage to let her love overcome my fear. Margot and I were married, and to my joy, we became a family. My children had gotten over the hurt and anger, and even they couldn't help but love Margot. My first wife moved on and found happiness with someone else. Margot and I built a life together even as her cancer returned and threatened again to take it away from us, and Margot showed me day in and day out that *love is stronger than fear.*

Love trumps fear, every time. She proved it to me over and over—in the way she loved me even as I let fear and guilt poison our happiness, despite the fact that it took me years to fully commit to being with her and that I was often too afraid to trust and let her in. She proved it in the way she stayed openhearted even when life threw cancer at her, in her refusal to ever give in to victimization, in the way she gave more and more love even as her body was wasting away. She chose to see cancer as a teacher, a blessing, an opportunity to grow, and she never succumbed to fear. Every new symptom of the disease, no matter how painful or humiliating, became for her a reason to love more, rather than a cause for complaint. She became richer in love each day. Every conversation ended with "I love you." This was how she triumphed over cancer, even as it triumphed over her body.

It had taken me many years to finally stop running and let my love for Margot triumph over my fear. Once I did and we were together, fully committed to each other and to the battle we were fighting for her life, I learned how to go with her to the other side of fear and pain. She helped me create the space to see my childhood wounds for what they were and to begin to heal. She taught me to give and receive love, free from the filter of fear. And together, we learned how to break through to oneness, serenity, peace, love, and gratitude at some of the hardest moments of her illness—devastating diagnoses, unbearable pain, physical breakdown.

"The spiritual journey," writes Marianne Williamson, "is the relinquishment—or unlearning—of fear and the acceptance of love back into our hearts."[20] As we learn to accept ourselves and our woundedness, to undo the programming of our parents and our teachers and our culture, we open the doors for love to melt away the scar tissue.

Against all odds, Margot survived many more years than any of her doctors expected. Three times the cancer came back, and three times she fought through to the other side. I believe deeply that it was our triumph over fear that kept the disease in check—the love and acceptance we were living and giving to each other.

Through all of this, I was opening and softening, but it was not until the final months before she passed that the walls around my heart fully broke down. And it was her death that chipped away the last pieces of debris. My heart was finally open, completely free to love and be loved, but my soul mate had left her physical body.

If there could have been a harder way to learn this lesson, I cannot imagine it. Some people seem to be able to learn gracefully, moving through their spiritual growth without intense suffering and tragedy. I guess I was a tough case. It took being given the greatest gift in the world and then losing it to fully break down the walls around my heart and return to the knowing I had as a child: that life is very simple, it is love. Everything is love. You and I are love. We are not the names our parents gave us; the fears our culture taught us; the achievements and possessions we accumulated; the wounds we buried deep inside. We are the limitless possibilities and energy of love. And in the end, love is always stronger than fear.

Living with No Regret

Grief, someone once said, is tough, but regret is much worse. Actually, the language was a little more colorful, but you get the idea. In learning to live with a truly open heart, one of the great challenges is to let go of regret and its ugly sister, guilt. These negative emotions go hand-in-hand with the fear that we are programmed to believe as children. They reinforce the walls around our hearts with feelings of unworthiness and shame, making it more difficult for us to freely give or receive love. Letting go of guilt and regret makes space for you to discover the extraordinary freedom that comes when we learn to forgive ourselves and accept what is.

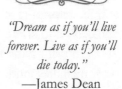

"Dream as if you'll live forever. Live as if you'll die today."
—James Dean

I grew up Catholic, so I know a thing or two about guilt. At school, we learned the difference between venial sin, mortal sin, and unpardonable sin. But guilt and regret don't just plague Catholics; they can afflict any of us at any point in life. It's a human tendency to dwell on the past and to judge ourselves harshly. The seductive thought "what if . . ." or the tempting whisper "if only . . ." can lure us into a parallel universe of how things could have been, a maze of twisting pathways and junctions in which we can wander for a lifetime. Regret and guilt trick us into believing that they are noble emotions. Even though they feel bad, we think they're good for us. In the throes of guilt and regret, we believe that we sincerely intend to do better in the future, to mend our ways, to try harder. The problem is, while we're feeling bad about the past and well-intentioned toward the future, we miss being here in the present moment. Regret and guilt create nothing but suffering for ourselves and for those who we neglect while we feel bad. As Calvin, the wise six-year-old star of Bill Watterson's *Calvin and Hobbes* comic strip, puts it, "There's no problem so awful that you can't add some guilt to it and make it even worse."[21]

I'm not saying that we shouldn't honestly learn from past mistakes and attempt to do better. Sometimes a "guilty conscience" or a sense of regret can trigger healthy self-examination and inspire genuine growth. Most of us have a sense of what's right and what's wrong, and our inner moral compass can help to guide us to improve ourselves. We can always endeavor to become better people than we were in the past, and if a moment of guilt helps us to do that, then it's doing a good thing. But that's different from getting lost in the feelings of guilt and regret and beating ourselves up for things that can't be undone. Giving too much attention to feeling guilty, or wishing that the past had been different, can actually slow down our growth and transformation. Learning to be at peace with the past— even if it looks like a long line of mistakes and failings—

is what allows us to be present in the present. In the end, those we love don't expect us to be perfect. But they do expect us to be present. We can cause tremendous pain and confusion in our relationships if we withdraw into the seemingly noble inner world of self-judgment and regret.

This has been one of the hardest lessons I've learned. Guilt is one of the earliest emotions I can remember—a kind of vague, undefined sense that if I were a better person, perhaps my father wouldn't behave in the ways he did. Perhaps he wouldn't drink so much, or yell and humiliate me, or turn a "spanking" into something worse. Like Woody Allen's character in *Broadway Danny Rose*, I felt guilty all the time, even though I never did anything to feel that guilty about. Later, when I actually had done plenty to feel guilty about, my guilt became cemented by regret. My self-destructive outbursts hurt those I loved and betrayed their trust. I wished I could take it all back, but the pain of those feelings more often led to another bout of self-destructive behavior than it did to real change or growth. Making oneself feel bad in the present moment for things one has done in the past only makes one more likely to repeat those behaviors. Once I broke the self-destructive cycle and started to create my life the way I wanted it, I experienced a period of respite from the whispers of guilt and regret.

When I met Margot and made the difficult choice to leave my marriage for a chance at new love, my demons, to my surprise, resurfaced with a vengeance. In a sense, throughout most of my time with Margot, I had my own cancer eating away at me. I don't mean to casually equate my psychological pain to the physical agony my beloved wife endured, but guilt is to the soul as cancer is to the body, slowly destroying it from inside. I felt guilty about the way I'd treated my former wife, Lisa, guilty about the suffering I'd caused my kids, guilty about how hard I'd made it for Margot. All of these feelings caused me to withdraw from Margot, setting in motion another cycle of guilt—this time fueled by regret that I'd not been there for her more fully when she first got sick. I constantly second-guessed the medical decisions we'd made, especially those from which I'd been absent, and agonized over the cost of the mistakes and delays that were beyond our control. In my darkest moments, I even blamed myself for her cancer—as if somehow the universe was teaching me a lesson that I was too stubborn to learn in any gentler way. And when she died, I was consumed by regret for all the times I chose something else over spending time with her, all the irrelevant things that I would now have traded a thousand times for just another minute with her, a single touch or kiss.

We tend to be tough on ourselves. I could have made a long list of all the things I did right, but my attention was more focused on those things I could have done better. It's a normal human tendency, but not a healthy one. When I spoke at Margot's memorial service, I ended with the most honest statement I could make at the time, baring my agonizing regret to my friends and family:

As I stand here before you today, brokenhearted, it is for two reasons. My best friend and soul mate has left Earth before me, and I will miss her every day until I can meet her beyond this world. And the second reason that I am heartbroken is that I could have been better, I could have listened better, I could have been more present, I could have looked in her eyes deeper, held her hand tighter. I could have told her she looked beautiful more often, I could have told her how much I loved her more often, I could have loved her better. I share this with you for only one reason, so that when your turn comes, as it will, your regrets will be a little less than mine and your heart will hurt a little bit less.

What I've learned, in the months and years since that day, is how to live without regret. I've discovered that there are two essential elements to living fully in the present moment, free from regret or guilt. I call these "living like there is no tomorrow" and "living like there is no yesterday."

Live like there is No Tomorrow

What would you do if you knew you were going to die tomorrow? It's become something of a cliché, but this question holds powerful

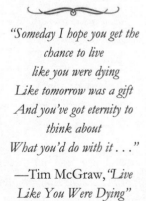

"Someday I hope you get the chance to live like you were dying Like tomorrow was a gift And you've got eternity to think about What you'd do with it . . ."

—Tim McGraw, *"Live Like You Were Dying"*

wisdom for all of us. We touched on this question in Chapter 2, with regard to its power to clarify our dreams. Contemplating what we would do in the face of certain and imminent death brings to the surface all those things we are putting off till tomorrow, all those things we wish we'd changed or set right, all the hopes and dreams we've been postponing, all the pleasures we've been denying ourselves.

Do it now! The foundation of a life with no regrets is to live as fully as possible in the moment, never putting off until tomorrow what you could do today. As Tim McGraw sings in his beautiful song on this theme, which I listen to almost every day, go skydiving or Rocky Mountain climbing. Take that vacation you've never found time to take. Tell people you love them. Say you're sorry and make up with those people from whom you've been estranged. Would you spend time wallowing in regret if you had only a day to live? Would you procrastinate about important tasks? Would you let pride or shame get in the way of mending a relationship? Of course not. You'd learn from the mistakes of the past, take full responsibility for your actions, and waste no time in being different.

"Each day is an opportunity to travel back into tomorrow's past and change it."

—Robert Brault, *Some Wit, Some Whimsy*

We can learn a lot about living from those who know they are dying. In her recent book *The Top Five Regrets of the Dying,* Australian palliative nurse Bronnie Ware shared what she has learned from sitting at the bedsides of numerous men and women as they were taking their last breaths. When asked about what they regretted or wished they had done differently, the people she spoke to came back again and again to a few key themes, which she summarized as follows:

Top Five Regrets of the Dying

1. I wish I'd had the courage to live a life true to myself, not the life others expected of me.

2. I wish I hadn't worked so hard.

3. I wish I'd had the courage to express my feelings.

4. I wish I had stayed in touch with my friends.

5. I wish that I had let myself be happier.

—From *The Top Five Regrets of the Dying*
by Bronnie Ware

Each of these common regrets point to a way you can live with more love, today—love for yourself and love for those around you. Take a few minutes to think about this list. If you were to die tomorrow, how many of these regrets would apply to you? And what could you start doing differently now to change that?

The first regret, which Ware cites as the most common, points to what we have been discussing in the opening chapters of this book: What is your dream? What is the life you are truly here to live, rather than the one that others expect you to live? It also encompasses the recognition that we all tend to be programmed by the expectations of others and of society, and are afraid of not conforming to those expectations. In the short-term this may bring approval or acceptance, but it is not a recipe for long-term happiness or fulfillment.

The second regret is an interesting one. Ware notes that this one came particularly from men, although she speculates that this may have been due to the generation of people she was speaking to, most of whom had grown up in a time when women were not the primary breadwinners. For those of us reading this today, it applies to anyone who spends all of their time and energy climbing the ladder of material success without taking time to enjoy the rewards it can bring. There's nothing wrong with working hard, but are you working on something that you are passionate about, something rewarding and energizing? And do you get to enjoy the fruits of your work in the present moment, or are they always postponed to the future?

The third regret speaks to our discussion in the previous chapter. Do you allow love to be stronger than fear? Do you freely express what you feel, or does fear of rejection, betrayal, or loss hold you back? Practice living each day by the rule that you don't want to go to bed with anything important unsaid. We tend to take relationships for granted, particularly those that are most important to us. Make it a daily habit to express gratitude to your loved ones, to honor and cherish your bonds, to communicate your love and respect for the people in your life. If you can live like this day to day, you are unlikely to find yourself on your deathbed regretting that you didn't have the courage to express your feelings.

The fourth regret is one I am sure we can all relate to, long before we find ourselves on our deathbeds. Do you make time to stay in touch with your friends?

Sometimes all it takes is a short phone call or a brief email, but it is all too easy to make the excuse that something else is more important. Next time that happens, ask yourself if that "something else" will be more important when you're lying on your deathbed. Pick up the phone, write the email. It irritated me when Margot would always answer her phone, but in hindsight I appreciate how much she cared for her friends and kept those connections alive and energized with love and support. That love would come back to her hundreds of times over when she lay dying.

The fifth regret on the list is a particularly poignant one. Do you allow yourself to be happy? Ware writes, "Many did not realize until the end that happiness is a choice. They had stayed stuck in old patterns and habits."[22] One of the most common habits that we use to deny ourselves the choice of happiness is our attachment to guilt and regret. Don't let yourself realize only on your deathbed that you let guilt and regret steal your happiness and cloud your ability to love.

"Holding on is believing that there's only a past; letting go is knowing that there's a future."
—Daphne Rose Kingma,
The Ten Things to Do When Your Life Falls Apart

Live Like There Is No Yesterday

Living like there is no tomorrow will no doubt make you a better, happier person, less likely to reach the end of your life with important things left undone or unsaid. But we are all human, and perfection is not in our nature.

No matter how hard we try to be a good person and do right by those we love, there is no way to avoid making mistakes or hurting people along the way. We cannot know what challenges life will confront us with and how we will respond. The second part of living without regret is, in my experience, harder than the first. It asks us to have the courage to let the past be—to accept what is and realize that we cannot change it. That's why I call this "living like there is no yesterday."

To heal and move through my grief, I had to be willing to stop judging myself for what I believed were my many shortcomings in my years with Margot. There was a part of me that believed that self-scrutiny, not forgiveness, would make everything all right, but the opposite has been true. I can now see that all the years I spent judging myself, feeling guilty, and burying my feelings of loneliness only led me to repeat those behaviors I felt worst about. I never thought that losing my wife would lead me to finally forgive myself, but it has, and I am grateful.

I used to think that true freedom and safety meant controlling or predicting everything. I caused a lot of pain by trying to control the people I loved and the circumstances of my life, and I expended a lot of energy trying to control myself and get rid of all the parts of myself that I didn't like. Learning to let go of control and accept reality was a terrifying task for me. But it turned out that freedom lay on the other side of that step. Freedom came from learning how to love it all—my mistakes and my shortcomings, Margot's sickness, and even her death. I learned to see it all as part of the perfection of life—to love "what is" rather than constantly fighting reality, insisting that it should be, or should have been, different.

I did not learn this lesson by myself. One of the guides to whom I am most grateful for her help following Margot's death was the spiritual teacher Byron Katie. I attended her nine-day School for The Work with her some months after Margot passed, which I'll speak about in more depth in the following chapter. Her essential message is that our suffering originates

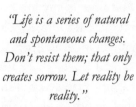

"Life is a series of natural and spontaneous changes. Don't resist them; that only creates sorrow. Let reality be reality."
—Lao Tzu, *Tao Te Ching*

from the ways in which our thoughts conflict with reality. "Wanting reality to be other than it is," she writes, "is hopeless. . . What you think shouldn't have happened *should* have happened. It should have happened because it did, and no thinking in the world can change that. This doesn't mean that you condone it or approve of it. It just means you can see things without resistance and without the confusion of your inner struggle."[23]

When we try to fight reality, to rewrite history and change what has already happened, we cause tremendous suffering to others and ourselves. Can we find the courage to let the past be the past, to live like there were no yesterday? It's not easy. Most of us tend to live life with one eye, if not both, glued to the rearview mirror, trying to rearrange the traffic behind us. It's no wonder that we continue to get into accidents in the present moment. Our attention is consumed with a futile quest to change what already is. How can we live and love, freely and fully, if we are distracted in this way? "When we stop opposing reality," Katie writes, "action becomes simple, fluid, kind, and fearless."[24] Letting go of guilt and regret frees our attention from the past, allowing us to love wholeheartedly in the present moment.

Since I've learned to stop fighting reality, for the first time in my life I am free of the torment of guilt and regret. I no longer believe that God or any higher power is judging me from on high, and I don't believe we should take that attitude with ourselves either. My religion has evolved into an understanding that whatever higher power exists in this universe, it only looks on us with love. Guilt, sin, and judgment are human inventions that we project onto the idea of God and then back onto ourselves.

The origin of the word "sin," in fact, is the Greek word *hamartia*, which simply means "to miss the mark" or "to miss the target." It was also used in Old English archery. It's not such a terrible thing to miss now and again. That's how we learn to shoot the arrow more accurately, straighter and truer, the next time. Misses and mistakes are part of life, as are human shortcomings, cancer, and death. Love, joy, connection, compassion, beauty, and generosity are also part of life.

I believe spirituality is an energy, a power, a source, that runs through everything. As hard as it may be to accept at times, everything is perfect the way it is. I know that what is done is done, and I cannot change it. We can strive to be the best we can be in each and every situation, and when it is done we can only let go. Reality is as it is, and there is no point in wasting our energy and stunting our ability to love by fighting a losing battle to change what cannot be changed. Learn from those who face impending death, and allow yourself to be happy. Live fully today, as if there were no yesterday and no tomorrow.

A Good Life

"To live in this world, you must be able to do three things: to love what is mortal; to hold it against your bones knowing your own life depends on it; and, when the time comes to let it go, to let it go."

—Mary Oliver,
Blackwater Woods

When Margot was taking her last breaths, she and I were blessed to be guided by a man who has dedicated his life to helping people die consciously and peacefully. Dale Borglum, founder of the Living/Dying Project, has helped hundreds if not thousands of people step through the veil that separates this world from whatever lies beyond it. But the greatest wisdom he shared with us was not really about death; it was about life. "There aren't really special tools or techniques one needs to learn in order to die well," Dale says. "It's exactly the same tools that will help one be fully alive: generosity, awareness, compassion, being grounded, being centered, having mercy for those in need. Those are the qualities that, when one is approaching death, will help one meet that event with openness and equanimity."[25]

I learned these lessons through losing someone I loved very much. I hope that those reading this book will not have to suffer that kind of loss to begin to live a life free from guilt and regret. However, sooner or later we all confront the reality of death. Sometimes it is tragic and unexpected, snatching a loved one from us before we have the chance to say goodbye. But sometimes we see it coming and have the opportunity to approach this transition consciously. Dale taught Margot and me the importance of being prepared for death, so that each person has the opportunity to say goodbye and let go.

We cannot know for sure what lies beyond the veil of death, and, depending on our religious beliefs, we may have very different ideas about this mystery. But many of the great religious traditions agree on certain things, which are confirmed by the experience of people who have taken one step beyond the veil and come back (so-called "near-death experiences"). In particular, it seems to be the case that the willingness of loved ones to let go and accept the impending death is critical to the dying person's ability to go in peace and transition freely to whatever comes next. Dale's work draws on this combined wisdom to help the dying prepare for what awaits them and to help those who are left behind to accept and consciously let go. You can learn more about Dale's work with the Living/Dying Project at www.livingdying.org.

If you, or someone you love, is confronting imminent death, I encourage you to meet this transition as consciously as possible. Denial, fueled by guilt or regret, only prolongs the agony—often literally. I saw this firsthand with my father, who remained in denial of my mother's death even when there was no possibility of her survival. She lay in a coma for seven days until he finally found the courage to let her go, after which she quickly passed from this world.

Whatever regrets you have, a deathbed is not the place to nurse them. Forgive yourself and others, so that you can give the final gift any human being gets to give another: the freedom to go in peace.

I think back to Dale's wisdom often as I go about my life without Margot. I don't know why the universe chose to take her away so soon. But I do know that what is done is done, and that if I can live my life with one-tenth of the grace with which she accepted her death, I will make a positive impact on this world.

Love Is Not Broken by Death

"No one ever told me that grief felt so like fear," wrote C.S. Lewis, in *A Grief Observed*.[26] It's true. There's really nothing anyone can do to prepare you for the terrifying reality of grief—for the days when you can't even get out of bed, the days when all you do is walk around in circles, the days when suicide seems like a welcome way out. Worst of all are the unanswerable questions: Why would my wife, fifteen years younger than me, die before me? How do I keep on living? What happens to those who die? And what happens to those of us who stay behind—to my heart, my spirit, my very existence? Is it possible to rise above this depth of brokenness?

> *"What we have once enjoyed we can never lose; All that we love deeply becomes a part of us."*
>
> —Helen Keller,
> *We Bereaved*

Margot's death tested everything I'd learned up to that point about the power of love. At first, I thought I'd lost love for good. I felt as if death had taken everything away and left me with nothing but pain, or at best, numbness. As time passed, however, I discovered that

93

her death was teaching me a new lesson about love. Margot's body was gone, but her love remained. I found her again in my own heart, in the compassion, openness, and care that I began to feel for everyone around me. I found her in the beauty of this world that she had loved so much, in the flaming crimson of the sunset and the cool glow of the harvest moon. I found her in the energy that I believe is the essence of everything in this universe and beyond. *Love is not broken by death.*

If you've ever lost someone you loved very deeply, you may have learned this lesson too. You may have felt the pain and numbness recede just enough to discover, to your amazement, the warmth and tenderness of a heart broken open. You may have seen the fog of grief clear just enough to glimpse a world more beautiful than before. Love never dies. It may be obscured, for some time, by the pain of loss, but it is always there. And when the one that you love is no longer here in a physical body, the love that you shared can evolve and expand in new ways.

My own realization of the enduring power of love came through the help of Tobe, my physical therapist, who had been treating me for a neck injury. Some weeks after Margot's death, I went for a session with him. He was a six-foot-tall, physically imposing guy, and there was no way I was letting on, even the littlest bit, how much I was falling apart. Of course, he saw right through my tough act and said something I've never forgotten:

"Margot came here and learned what she was supposed to learn and did what she was supposed to do, and left. And you should celebrate that. You, on the other hand, are still here, so you either have something

94

to do or something to learn. You should be excited about that."

Excited? Nothing could have been further from describing how I felt. But I heard him, through the grief and pain, and I instinctively knew that he was right. I couldn't give up. I needed to find out why I was still here. I needed to do something, anything, to find a way forward. I knew that Tobe had been deeply influenced by the spiritual teacher Byron Katie, whose work I mentioned in the previous chapter, and when he suggested that I sign up for her nine-day school in Los Angeles, I decided to do so, despite the fact that I had shunned anything that sounded like school since I had been kicked out of the eighth grade.

Much of those nine days is a blur in my memory, but three moments stand out crystal clear. The first occurred during one of the daily "morning walks." Katie, as everyone calls her, had given all 250 participants instructions to walk in silence down Century Boulevard near LAX each morning and pretend that nothing in the world had ever been named before. As we walked, we were to rename everything we saw. This seemed ridiculous to me at first, but on the second day, I found myself unexpectedly appreciating the power of the exercise. I don't know where the idea came from, but I chose to name every inanimate object "peace." The buildings, the bench, the bus driving past—all of these were peace. Every living thing, other than humans, I named "love." The birds, the sun, the earth, the sky—all of these were love. And human beings I named "joy." Everything I saw went into one of these three categories: peace, love, or joy.

As I walked around a corner, out of the shadow of the hotel and into the morning sunlight, I saw a beautiful white airplane coming in to land, floating through a clear blue sky, carrying people to the city. In my eyes, what I was seeing was *peace, floating on love, carrying joy*. No matter what happens, I'd told myself, I can come back to this moment and know that everything is peace, love, and joy. I do this now when situations or people get difficult. I remember that moment and once again I am awash in peace, love, and joy. Try it for yourself—it's a simple and easy way to remind yourself of the essential goodness of this world.

The second powerful insight came when Katie asked us to do an exercise that involved writing out our love stories. I wrote about Margot, filling many pages with descriptions of our life together. When we were done, she asked us to go through and strike out all the adjectives and exaggerations. In my story, there were plenty. Then she had us take out any unnecessary detail, any personal feelings, drama, and so on, until we had pared down the story to its essence. Mine went from several pages to just one sentence. Here's what it said:

> *Man meets woman; they learn about love; she dies; man tries to go on.*

I learned from this exercise that we all have a story, and we all think that our particular story is unique— more dramatic, more tragic, more challenging, or more exciting than everyone else's. When we hold on to our stories, attached to their emotional drama and personal meaning, we separate ourselves from each other and from being present in the moment. I encourage you to try this exercise as well. Write your story, as fully and authentically as you can. Don't censor or limit your expression. Then go through and remove all the adjectives. Remove all your thoughts about it, all your feelings, all your conclusions, all your beliefs. Remove all unnecessary detail. Then see what's left. Paring your story down to its essence, stripping away the emotion and the drama and the detail, can help you to understand that you aren't alone.

The last exercise, which had the greatest impact on me, was using Byron Katie's central teaching exercise— the four questions she calls "The Work"—to examine the excruciating fact of my wife's death. The four questions, which she teaches people to use to inquire into thought that is causing them to suffer, are simple:

"The Work" by Byron Katie – 4 Essential Questions

1. Is it true? (Yes or no. If no, move to 3.)
2. Can you absolutely know that it's true? (Yes or no.)
3. How do you react, what happens, when you believe that thought?
4. Who would you be without the thought?

Visit Byron Katie's website at www.thework.com *to learn more and download free worksheets to try it yourself. You may be amazed by the results!*

For me, the thought that tortured me, day in and day out, was, "My wife died." This one thought obliterated all others, so I had no choice but to apply The Work to this. "It takes a great deal of courage to see through the story of a death," Katie said. "Let's investigate, if you're up for it, and see if it's possible to end the war with reality."[27] Feeling I had nothing left to lose, I applied the four questions to this thought.

Is it true? I took myself mentally back to Margot's room and visualized her lying on the bed, the oxygen tube attached to her, the chemotherapy port protruding from her bald head. Her mother is sitting on one side; I am sitting on the other. Her mother grabs for her pulse, and there is nothing. I put my ear to her heart. Her sister turns off the loud oxygen machine in the next room so we can hear if she is breathing. Silence. Her body died. I was there. I saw them take her away. I read the death certificate. Yes, she is dead.

Can you absolutely know it's true? I took myself back there again, replaying the facts in my mind. I had no doubt her body died. She stopped breathing. Her heart stopped. But wait—I felt her presence even after her body was still. I felt her with me and continued to feel her in the days and weeks since. Could I know absolutely that she died? Suddenly there was a crack of uncertainty.

How do you react, what happens, when you believe that thought? Immediately, I'm back in the fog. Lonely, depressed, suicidal. I don't want to live anymore if she's gone.

Who would you be without that thought? I'd be free from pain. I'd have energy again; I'd have hope. I'd be able to go on with my life.

Once you've been through these four questions, the final part of The Work is what Katie calls "the turnaround." This simply means you take the thought and turn it around so it becomes its opposite. And then you find genuine examples of how that opposite statement is in fact true. There are a few ways you can do this. In this case, one possible turnaround was, "My wife didn't die." I looked for examples that would show this to be true. I feel her in my heart. Her love is still with me, so she didn't die. Then I tried a further turnaround. Rather than switching a negative to a positive, another technique is to replace the other person with oneself. In this case, the turnaround would be, "I died." That might sound like a strange thing to say, but when I looked for examples of it being true, something resonated with me. A part of me *had* died when Margot passed.

It was as if all of my fear, negativity, self-destructiveness, and selfishness had just been burned out by grief. What was left was softer and less clearly defined. I didn't yet know what form this "new me" would take, but I knew that much of the "old me" had gone. Sometime later, I came across a beautiful passage by the spiritual teacher Ram Dass, which put the experience into words far more eloquently than I could. After suffering a debilitating stroke, he published a book called *Still Here,* in which he writes that

> *. . . when you "bear the unbearable," something within you dies. My identity flipped over and I said, "So that's who I am—I'm a soul!" I ended up looking at the world from the Soul level as my ordinary, everyday state. And that's grace....*

When you're secure in the soul, what's to fear? Since the stroke, I can say to you with an assurance I haven't felt before, that faith and love are stronger than any changes, stronger than aging, and, I am very sure, stronger than death.[28]

When I read this description, it resonated with me. It was as if Margot's death stripped away much of the debris of my old self and left me with a surprising gift of deeper faith and love.

Katie's simple process helped me come to this realization. Those four questions are very powerful. I'd suggest starting with a simpler thought than a death if you can—something more along the lines of, "My brother is mad at me," or, "I'm a failure at my job." The seemingly irrevocable reality of death is a challenge to turn around. But if you have been unfortunate enough to lose someone you loved deeply, you may also find that these questions can help you be a little freer of the conviction that your loved one is gone forever. As Katie says, "Through self-inquiry, we can see that only love remains."[29]

"Reality is always kinder than the story we tell ourselves about it. If I were to tell the story of reality, it would have to be a love story."

—Byron Katie, *A Thousand Names for Joy*

Death Is Only a Doorway

Only love remains. Margot knew this before she passed. In her final months, I saw her go through an extraordinary transformation, slowly letting go of her attachment to everything until all that was left was love—radiant love shining through the pain in her eyes, more love than could be contained by her bruised and broken body. Through watching her, I began to understand, more deeply, the traditional spiritual teachings on letting go of attachment. The Buddha said that attachment is the root of all suffering, and he advised his followers to let go of all attachments. I could never relate to this teaching. It always seemed to me that letting go of attachments would result in a state of not caring or not feeling. Margot demonstrated quite the opposite. Letting go, for her, didn't mean she stopped loving or cherishing those around her. She let go of her attachment to any idea of the way things "should be," to any particular form her life should take, even to her physical body. And in letting go of all these attachments, she made space to love without conditions. Her love was amplified as she let go.

That's how she was able to embrace her cancer without fear and meet her death with extraordinary grace and openness. "I curse the disease, but it has not always cursed me," she wrote on her blog. "Now I will never be afraid of it as it has taken me to the edge of my reality." A few months before her death, she expressed a similar sentiment in a text message to my daughter Michelle: "Cancer is a curse in so many ways, but it's been my greatest blessing. . . . I'm not scared; I was born to have this path and destiny. I'm proud to call it mine. I love my cancer because it was there as the miracle of life was unfolding."

We shared the belief that death is not the end but simply a doorway to whatever comes next. My conviction in this was severely tested by the event of her death, but over time it only deepened. I remember a time, a few months before, when Margot and I were flying back from Los Angeles after one of her many hospital visits. I held her covered bald head in my arms for most of the flight. At one point she looked at me and asked, "Is this the end?" My immediate response was, "No, honey, this is just a bump in the road." Then I felt as if I'd been dishonest, because I didn't know if this was the end. So I told her what I truly believed: "Honey, the universe is like a giant Disney World and planet Earth is just one of the rides. There is no end, just more rides."

That was the most honest answer I could give her, and it's still my belief today. I don't believe death is an end. I believe our souls come here to Earth in order to learn what we need to learn and to evolve in the ways we need to evolve. We come here to learn about love. And then we go home to wherever we came from, until we are ready to learn our next set of lessons. I choose to call that home "heaven," but my beliefs are not limited to a Christian or even a religious framework. Margot's belief in this enabled her to face death without fear, with an open heart and a peaceful mind. And in fact, I believe that she reached out from beyond the veil of death to confirm to me and others she loved that this was true. That may sound farfetched or superstitious, but I believe the events I'm about to share with you are more than

"The mark of your ignorance is the depth of your belief in injustice and tragedy. What the caterpillar calls the end of the world, the Master calls the butterfly."

—Richard Bach, *Illusions*

just coincidence.

The Butterfly Effect

Let me preface these stories by saying that Margot loved butterflies. Their colorful beauty and joyful energy were a source of great delight to her. When we would go hiking together, she could lay in a meadow and watch them for hours.

A couple of days before Margot passed, my sister Stacy took a hiking trip to Yosemite. She had thought long and hard about whether to go, but the hospice staff was confident that Margot had a few more days, so Stacy reluctantly left her side to spend a few days with her husband in the beautiful wilderness. The next morning, as they were approaching the final climb to the top of Half Dome, Stacy's husband saw that he had a missed call from my daughter. He had no signal to retrieve the message, but as they looked at each other they both wondered if this was it. On the hike back, they listened to the message and learned that Margot had gone.

Consumed with grief and regret, Stacy hiked ahead of her friends. When they caught up to her on the trail, they noticed that Stacy was staring at a beautiful butterfly that was flying around her knees. Looking at the butterfly, she thought of Margot and sensed that although she had left her body she was happy and at peace. But she was still sad that she had not been there to say goodbye. Half a mile later, as they crossed a stream, they noticed the same butterfly was following them. Without warning, it flew close to Stacy's face and hovered there, almost looking into her eyes. And then it flew off into the spaciousness of Yosemite Valley, beautiful and blissful. Stacy let go of her regret. She knew she had been right where she was supposed to be at the moment Margot took her last breath. And she knew that Margot was not gone, but had simply transitioned into the next stage of her journey, like a caterpillar transforms into a butterfly.

Stacy was not the only one to receive this message. The day after Margot died, my son Christopher also encountered a beautiful butterfly as he was rock climbing with a friend on Mount Diablo. It landed on his rope, right in front of him, and he too said that it seemed to look right into his eyes. In that moment, he felt Margot's presence. Later I would discover that the trail he was hiking was in fact right above the new house that Margot and I had purchased together right before she died and that she had never had the chance to move into.

When I heard these stories, I felt sure that my wife was communicating to us through these beautiful creatures she loved so much. She was telling us that death was simply a doorway to her next adventure. But I wondered, why hadn't she visited me? All day long I walked around asking everyone, "Where is my butterfly story? Where is my butterfly story?" Then that evening, at 10:00 p.m., I received a text message from a salesperson I didn't even know who works at my car dealership. Attached was a photo of a beautiful butterfly that had flown into the dealership and settled behind her desk, about as close as it could get to my office, which had its door closed. It stayed there until she gently escorted it back out into the sunshine. No one before or since has seen a butterfly in that building. I later learned that this type of butterfly is called a mourning butterfly. I keep a framed photo of it in my office to remind me of the message that I am convinced the universe was trying to give me that day: love never dies.

Just a couple of days later, one of Margot's dear friends in Los Angeles, unaware of these stories, posted the following quote from writer Melanie Moushigian Koulouris on her Facebook page:

> *Butterflies are a representation of the cycle of life, an example of the true beauty of the physical and spiritual journey we all experience and venture through. We start out helpless and new to the world, eventually embracing change, blossoming into a magnificent, colorful, one-of-a-kind creation with a world of possibilities and freedom to explore all that life endures. Spread your wings and fly . . .*

Margot's life with me and her love for me brought me my deepest sorrow and my greatest gift—the gift of transformation. Just as a caterpillar becomes a butterfly, I have been transformed as well. As I watched Margot go from temporary form to eternal and formless, from human to angel, I received the greatest gift of my life—the gift of transformation and the evolution of my soul. She allowed me to spread my wings and fly.

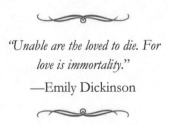

"Unable are the loved to die. For love is immortality."

—Emily Dickinson

From Grief to Giving

Is there life after death? This question takes on a new meaning after the loss of a loved one. Is there life for the one left behind? How do we find purpose, meaning, and direction when it feels like half of our soul has been ripped away? How do we find the will to get up and go on, to make plans and build a future, when the person we were supposed to share it with has left this world?

"When we descend all the way to the bottom of a loss, and dwell patiently, with an open heart, in the darkness and pain, we can bring back up with us the sweetness of life and the exhilaration of inner growth."

—Elizabeth Lesser,
Broken Open

After Margot passed, I felt like I'd lost my reason to get out of bed every day. For the first few weeks, I often didn't. In my darkest moment, I took too many sleeping pills and begged God to take me too so that I could be with her. But I woke up, still here, still alone. Even once I had realized that Margot's love—which was the essence of who she was—had not died, I still missed her physical presence so much that my life, at times, felt pointless without her. I couldn't imagine a future in which she was not there beside me, radiant and beautiful. For the previous nine years, helping her fight cancer had become my overriding purpose in life. Now I felt cast adrift. I kept remembering Tobe's words: "Margot came here and learned what she was supposed to learn and did what she was supposed to do, and left. And you should celebrate that. You, on the other hand, are still here, so you either have something to do or something to learn. You should be excited about that."

What was I still here to learn and do? Instinctively, I felt that Margot's death had shown me what I was here to learn: that love is the essence of everything, and love never dies. But what was I meant to do? I didn't know. Sometimes I couldn't imagine doing anything. This was profoundly out of character for me. For the first time in my life I had no impetus to run away from things or run toward things. I just stopped. I could hardly remember the last time I hadn't been busy controlling everything—trying to save her, trying to find answers, trying to hold my businesses together, trying to hold myself together. Now I stood still, unable to reconcile the paradox that love was here but she was gone. And unable to answer the question, "What am I here to do?"

"One cannot get through life without pain. . . . What we can do is choose how to use the pain life presents to us."
—Bernie S. Siegel, M.D, *Peace, Love, and Healing*

I would discover my answer in the most unlikely of places—somewhere I had hoped I would never find myself again. Only eighteen months after Margot's passing, I found myself sitting beside another deathbed, where a woman I had come to love dearly was struggling to breathe. The woman whose hand I was holding was the same age as Margot had been, and the same disease was ravaging her body. But that was where the resemblance ended. Amanda was a mother of three, as feisty, exuberant, and contentious as Margot had been graceful, dignified, and accepting. And while Margot had been privileged to be treated at the very best hospitals by the top specialists in the country, Amanda had struggled for many years without all of the resources to get the treatment she needed.

I'd first heard of Amanda a couple months before Margot died, when my friend Jim, Amanda's brother-in-law, contacted me asking for a referral to a good oncologist. Amanda had moved to the Bay Area to live with him and her sister in the hope that she could get better treatment. I had made the referral but then forgot about it, consumed by the pain and love of Margot's final weeks.

Soon after Margot's passing, in the grip of devastating grief, I wasn't capable of doing very much, but as the weeks passed, I remembered Amanda and started visiting her. I figured that my nine years of experience around breast cancer might be useful, and as I felt that I had nothing else meaningful to do, I started going to doctors' appointments with her and accompanying her when she went in for her surgeries. We became friends, sharing many deep conversations about the meaning of life and death. I couldn't be there for her as much as I wanted to be, because I was fighting my own demons of grief and regret at times, but it was in those hours we spent together, waiting in hospitals, taking walks around her neighborhood, that my new purpose was born.

I remember the day it began. We were sitting in an oncologist's office, as I'd done so many times with Margot. The doctor gave Amanda a grim prognosis: Stage 4 breast cancer. She would fight it with aggressive treatment until she would eventually succumb to the disease. No one could say for sure how long she would live, but it appeared her time was short. The doctor explained that the best protocol to extend her life at all would be a combination of three types of chemotherapy. Like Margot, Amanda had no other desire than to fight for each day so she could remain here with her children and her loved ones for as long as possible. Then the doctor said something I'll never forget: "But your insurance will only pay for one, so that is all I can give you."

To be honest, I was taken aback. Cushioned by wealth and privilege, in all of Margot's battles we'd never encountered this enemy. We had had the best private medical insurance we could get and plenty of supplemental income when needed. Amanda, on the other hand, had only Medicare, and very little money. Before this moment, I'd hardly considered how many people fight not only cancer, but the unfairness of a system that gives rich people access to the best treatment and denies those with less fortunate circumstances a chance at survival or at least a few more months of life. Outraged at this injustice, I simply handed the doctor my credit card and said, "Give this woman whatever she needs." It was in that moment, in that act, that a seed was planted—the seed of a mission to help people who don't have resources or great insurance and are fighting a terminal illness. My spontaneous gesture to help Amanda would later blossom into the Love From Margot Foundation—a nonprofit I established in 2012, just a few months after this experience.

Amanda remained a friend and an inspiration during her last few months. Accompanying her to doctors' visits, I continued to be shocked by the ways people talked down to her or subtly implied that she was not worthy of the treatment she was getting. I got to know her family: her sister, Marian; her three beautiful children, aged twenty, eighteen, and nine; and her baby granddaughter; along with many other members of her very large family. I watched her struggle with the pain of leaving them behind and her fear of death. And finally, I sat at her bedside as she labored, unconscious, to take her final breaths. She fought for every gasp of air during those last days of her life, surrounded by her sisters, her children, her granddaughter, her brother-in-law, her cousins.

There was nothing peaceful about Amanda's deathbed. She lay in a hospital bed in the living room of her sister's house. All around her, chaos reigned. Dogs played around and under the bed. The family talked nonstop, trying to make sense of this sad picture unfolding before their eyes, perhaps confronting their own mortality while Amanda prepared to transition into the next dimension. And of course there were a great deal of tears being shed openly. All the while, children played and laughed, oblivious to the full reality of the situation. The television blared, competing with Amanda's favorite Christian songs playing loudly from an iPod dock by her bed. She is dying, not going deaf, I remember thinking, but because she had lost consciousness, everyone in the family seemed to think it necessary to shout when speaking to her. Grief, anger, denial, and fear mingled with acceptance and love. It was not an easy place to be. After I spent a few hours there, I called my friend Dale from the Living and Dying Project. I was in despair—what could I do in the midst of this to help Amanda die a peaceful and dignified death? Dale told me, "Don't worry. Just go there with an open, loving, compassionate heart, and something will happen."

So I stopped worrying about the situation and allowed the chaos to flow around me as I sat in a kitchen chair next to her bed. I don't know if she knew I was there. Calling to mind everything I'd learned with Margot and from Dale, I sat at her bedside, with my right index finger gently stroking her hand for hours at a time. If my finger got tired, I'd change hands. I simply focused my attention on being present with an open, loving heart. I visualized the love from my heart meeting the love in her heart and the light in my soul meeting the light of her soul, uniting us beyond any separation.

For the first time in my life, I was fully present, loving, and being of service, undistracted by anything else. I hadn't been able to be fully present for Margot—I was too attached, too racked with fear and guilt, too terrified of losing her to allow myself to lose myself. With Amanda, although I loved her dearly and was sad to see her go, I was not attached like I was to Margot.

Sitting at Amanda's bedside, it was as if I dissolved. I became pure presence, pure attention, pure compassion. I thought I was blessing her, but it turned out that she was blessing me. To my surprise, a tremendous energy started to flow through my body, surging into and through my broken heart, then flooding up and down my spine. It was as if I were waking up suddenly from a long sleep. I could feel my cells starting to vibrate with aliveness and presence. After Amanda's spirit had left this world, she gave me the greatest gift of all: an overwhelming sense of purpose.

The slowly awakening care that had moved me to help Amanda now turned into a torrent of fierce compassion and intolerance for injustice. As I told my family at the time, trying to explain what had happened to me, I felt like an oak barrel with no top or bottom, being hurtled down a raging river. The desire to serve and to do good was surging through me, wiping out any last vestiges of fear or selfishness or regret or grief. I now knew the answer to the question that had been plaguing me. What was I here to do? It was simple: I was here to love and to serve. The sense of purpose was almost frightening in its intensity, but it was also the most liberating experience of my life. I knew I had no choice—my life was no longer my own. It belonged to those who needed my help.

To be honest, in the days and weeks following Amanda's death, as I worked to build my foundation and help other people in the Bay Area who were suffering from cancer and other life-threatening illnesses, I kept waiting for my old self to come back—for the fear, self-doubt, and despair to resurface. But that didn't happen.

Day after day, both Margot's and Amanda's presences were with me, inspiring me, encouraging me. The energy just kept flowing through me, bubbling up from the bottomless reservoir of love that is the essence of life itself.

When I spoke at Amanda's memorial, I told her friends and family about the incredible gift she had given me. I explained to them how Margot's life and death and her love for me taught me what love is and broke open my heart, while Amanda's death released me from myself and freed me to serve. I assured them, "Her life will continue, but more importantly, her love will continue, because she inspired me and she inspired this foundation." And I shared with them the clarity and simplicity of my newly awakened purpose: "Once you come to the realization that all that is real and all that matters is love, then there is only one thing you can do, and that is to serve."

Since then, the Love From Margot Foundation has helped numerous people in and around the San Francisco Bay Area who are suffering from breast cancer or other terminal diseases. We've helped with medical bills, mortgage payments, or nursing care to help someone die in peace at home.

> *"I have found the paradox that if you love until it hurts, there can be no more hurt, only more love."*
>
> —Mother Teresa

I'm busy every day responding to those who need my help. But in the midst of the busyness, I'm at peace. It's hard to explain, but when I learned the Sanskrit word *shanti,* which means "the peace that passes all understanding," I knew exactly what it meant. That was the gift Amanda had given me: the peace that accepts *what is* while all around it the river of compassion and care and service flows freely.

In a strange synchronicity, one of Amanda's daughters was named Shanti. And shortly after Amanda died, I was introduced to the executive director of a San Francisco–based organization called the Shanti Project, which has been helping people with cancer and HIV/AIDS for the past forty years. The Shanti Project wanted to partner with my foundation to help more people throughout California as well as throughout the country. This gave me an opportunity to serve for which I am deeply grateful. When I see these seeming coincidences, I can't help feeling that Margot and Amanda are still working to guide me in my newfound purpose.

Looking back, I can hardly believe how much has happened in the short time since Margot took her last breath and I wished that I could go with her. Grief has given way to immense gratitude, and while I miss my beautiful wife every day, I now know why I am here and feel blessed to have this opportunity to make a difference in the lives of others. In the process, my own life has been transformed. For the first time in my adult life I feel whole inside, rather than broken and incomplete. My days have meaning and purpose as never before. All the energy I once used up trying to fix, manipulate, and control life has now been freed up to simply love.

The quickest way to get out of grief, pain, despair, or anything that troubles you is simply to give. It's easy to be lost in your own suffering until you meet someone who is in a worse situation than you are. And believe me, if you sincerely try, you can always find someone worse off than you. There's an old saying: "I used to think I was bad off because I had no shoes until I met a man who had no feet." When you're feeling like life is hard and you're getting a raw deal, try thinking about another person and that person's problems rather than your own.

Margot always practiced this—even as she was fighting for her own life, she thought of others. In one of her blog updates, which were read by all of our friends and family in the last months of her life, she asked everyone reading it to "make an attempt today to move love and energy into a place in your life where you think you need it, or more importantly, where somebody else needs it." She requested that those sending love and good wishes to her also pray for others she knew who were suffering from the same disease—a boy facing major surgery, a woman with the same breast cancer and with whom she had been corresponding online. In her worst moments, she would think about the beggars we had seen in India, blind or missing limbs, and remember that she was not as bad off as some.

I'll never forget one night, right before she died, when she was in unbearable pain. The medications weren't working. I was in Las Vegas on a business trip, and she texted me in panic. I called her mother to get an ambulance before getting on the first plane home. In the process, running with my heavy bag, I ruptured a disc in my neck. In agony, I joined Margot in the ER and lay down on the floor. Despite her own unbearable pain, Margot threatened to get out of bed and leave unless the hospital staff brought me a bed. Even two days before she died, she was worrying about *my* pain, which could not have been a fraction of her own, and offered to give me a massage to ease my neck.

In caring for others, you forget yourself. In service, you lose yourself and your story. As I learned from Byron Katie, the greatest source of suffering is our attachment to our stories. If you are able to be fully there with someone else who is suffering, you get out of your story and discover that on the other side of your story is peace and freedom.

The Purpose of Life Is to Serve

Since time immemorial, human beings have contemplated the meaning of life. Unlike the other species with whom we share this beautiful blue-green planet, we have been blessed (or cursed) with a need for meaning, a desire to make sense out of things, a curiosity about why we are here. What is the purpose of life? There are many different ways to answer this question, and many who

"I slept and I dreamed that life is all joy. I woke and I saw that life is all service. I served and I saw that service is joy."

—Rabindranath Tagore

insist there is no answer to be found. The history of religious and philosophical thought can be seen as revolving largely around this question.

Sitting at Amanda's bedside, I felt blessed to be given an answer. *The purpose of life is to serve.* I was finally fulfilling the promise I'd made and broken in my early life and was discovering a beautiful truth: that meaning is found in the act of giving. This is by no means a new discovery—in fact, it is a theme we can trace back through many of the great religious and humanist

119

traditions. It's also an insight that is supported by modern psychology. A 2012 study from Stanford University investigating happiness and meaning came to the conclusion that among study participants (400 Americans aged 18 to 78), "meaningfulness went with being a giver rather than a taker."[30] I humbly offer my own experience and perspective on this simple but powerful realization, along with some of the stories, writings, and insights that have most inspired me, in the hope that they may inspire others to embrace a life of giving.

As we discussed in Chapter 2, many of us have been brought up to pursue happiness, as our Founding Fathers decreed. But happiness is a highly subjective and elusive state, one that tends to slip from one's grasp when pursued for its own sake. As holocaust survivor Victor Frankl, author of the classic *Man's Search for Meaning,* wrote, "It is the very pursuit of happiness that thwarts happiness."[31] Frankl, who chose to stay in his native Vienna to care for his parents rather than escape, was sent to a concentration camp where he lost his entire family, including his pregnant wife. He went through more suffering than most of us can imagine, but he came out the other side with an extraordinary perspective on what it means to live a meaningful life. He found meaning in what we can contribute, to others or to the world. "A man who becomes conscious of the responsibility he bears toward a human being who affectionately waits for him, or to an unfinished work . . . knows the 'why' for his existence and will be able to bear almost any 'how.'"[32]

Happiness, Frankl concluded, "cannot be pursued; it must ensue."[33] In other words, happiness is a by-product of living a purposeful and meaningful life. He also wrote, "being human always points, and is directed, to something or someone other than oneself. . . . The more one forgets himself—by giving himself to a cause to serve or another person to love— the more human he is."[34] A meaningful life, as the Stanford study confirms, comes from being a giver.

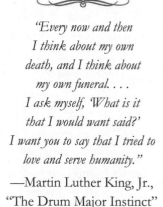

"Every now and then I think about my own death, and I think about my own funeral. . . . I ask myself, 'What is it that I would want said?' I want you to say that I tried to love and serve humanity."

—Martin Luther King, Jr., "The Drum Major Instinct"

Becoming a Giver

What does it mean to become a giver? Many of us tend to have an idea of what giving means—donating a lot of money to charity or volunteering a lot of time to help those less fortunate. We may feel guilty that we don't live up to that ideal, or we look forward to the day when we are no longer so busy trying to make ends meet and we will have the extra money or the free time to do so. However, too often our ideas of what giving might mean in the future can blind us to what we could be giving right now. As Irish politician and philosopher Edmund Burke wrote, "Nobody makes a greater mistake than he who did nothing because he could only do a little."

The idea that we don't have enough right now to give anything to others is a powerful mindset. Most of us have grown up in a culture fueled by the unconscious conviction that there's not enough to go around. So we feel driven to get as much as we can for ourselves and hold on to it—whether it be money, possessions, time, love, or attention. Of course, there are far too many people in this world who live in conditions of actual scarcity, and you may be one of them. I'm not suggesting that we should deny our own real needs or those of our family. But for many more of us, scarcity is more a mindset than an actual condition. We're convinced there is something "missing," and if we could just fill that void, we'd be free to give to others. "We live with scarcity as an underlying assumption," writes Lynn Twist in *The Soul of Money*.[35] And she points out the telling fact that this mindset of "not enough" and "more is better" afflicts the rich as much as it does the poor. That kind of void can never be filled by more possessions, as I found out when I got everything I wanted and still wasn't happy.

This mindset is hard to dislodge. By numerous measures, the standard of living in the United States has clearly risen over the past fifty years. But are we happier? It seems to me that the cultural craving for more has not lessened at all. And even those who have more than enough money feel the lack of other things just as acutely. I know plenty of millionaires who are miserable, still seeking to fill that hole in the soul.

What I discovered, as have many others, is that the only way to fill that void is to stop trying to do so and go in the completely opposite direction. Start giving. If you don't have money to spare, give of your time. Give your knowledge—share what you've learned or discovered with others. Give someone your full attention for the duration of a conversation. Give a smile to a stranger when you don't really feel like it. There are countless ways to become a giver and to discover the abundance of love that starts to flow through your life when you replace a mindset of scarcity with one of generosity.

Ideally, when you start to create the life of your dreams, build the act of giving into the intentions you set for yourself, as we discussed in Chapter 2. Don't let it be just an afterthought or a byproduct of wealth and success; make it part of your definition of success. This way you will ensure a life of meaning and purpose.

The Healing Power of Love

Ultimately, I believe that the greatest gift any of us can give—greater than money or objects or even time— is love. Freely given love is the most powerful force in the universe. Margot always believed in the power of love, and my faith was strengthened a hundredfold in the months leading up to her death by an experiment we tried. Margot was convinced that if enough love and intention was focused on her healing, she could beat the odds and survive that last battle with cancer, despite her doctors' gloomy prognosis. We set up a website called Send Margot Love, where we had a "prayer schedule" that all of her friends and family, and even strangers, could use to sign up for five-minute slots in which they would focus on sending her love, healing energy, and prayers. Our goal was to have people praying for her twenty-four hours a day. The response was remarkable, and the knowledge that so many people were thinking of her, as well as all the comments and postings on the website, were such a source of uplifting strength for Margot.

You may wonder how this strengthened my faith, given that she died anyway. Our prayers may not have been able to save her life, but I am convinced they had a huge effect on her. Over and over, she surprised her doctors with her responsiveness to treatments that they had little hope would work. I still remember the surprise on her oncologist's face when a test on a vial of her cerebral spinal fluid showed only two cancer cells, down from one hundred. She was convinced this was due to all the prayers being said for her. And whenever she had moments that were miraculously free from pain without the aid of medication, she attributed them to the energy of love that was flowing her way. Every morning that she woke up alive was a miracle to her. "Each one of you who has given me a second of gracing me with your energy has saved my life," she wrote in one of her blog updates. "I have been showered with more grace and compassion than I can ever explain."

Margot loved life and fully believed that love could heal her. But she also knew that it might simply be her time to go. "I joyfully accept any and all outcomes," she wrote, "because I also believe, feel, and know that my soul is eternal and that whenever my creator chooses for me to leave the confines of my body and the planet Earth to return to my permanent home, I will be ready, because I do believe we are all spiritual souls having an earthly experience so that we can become just a little more enlightened and that much closer to our creator."

In the end, it was indeed time for her to leave the confines of her battered body, but I have no doubt that those last seven months we had together—so full of pain and suffering and yet so transfused with love—were a gift from all those who loved and prayed for her.

You may think this sounds like superstition, but it's a topic that many people take very seriously. Numerous studies have been conducted on the power of prayer or "distant healing intention" as Marilyn Schlitz, President Emeritus and Senior Fellow of the Institute of Noetic Sciences, calls it. While the results are open to interpretation and often hotly debated, there is persuasive evidence for, at the very least, not dismissing the possibility that prayer can impact physical conditions. And if you're not religious and feel uncomfortable with the idea of prayer, just think in terms of energy and love. As one of our medical doctors said to me at the time, "What is prayer if not a form of love?"

On our foundation's website, we have set up a prayer schedule for the clients we serve. Visitors to the site can sign up to pray and/or send loving, healing energy to the clients. My iPhone is programmed every day at 8:00 a.m. to alert me to pray for our clients. I also use this time to pray for my family and anyone else I know that needs love and support. If prayer does nothing else, it gets me centered and allows me to focus on others for a minimum of five minutes, bringing me peace for that time. Do I believe that it actually works for those I send my energy to? While I may not be able to prove it, I have no doubt that beginning my day full of peace and love can only have a positive effect in this world.

Experiment with the power of love. Pick a situation in your life that you feel needs healing. Take a period of time each day, even just five minutes, and focus the energy of your love on that situation. You can even pick something within yourself—a wound, fear, or anxiety that is troubling you. Imagine enveloping that situation or inner challenge with loving, healing energy and undivided attention. If prayer is something you feel comfortable with, pray for healing. Don't try to figure it out or fix it—just love it. After you've been doing this for a week or two, look and see if there has been a change. You may be surprised by the results.

Giving of Yourself

Sometimes service comes down to simply being available to another person, giving him or her your full attention. I heard a beautiful story that illustrates this principle when I attended volunteer training at the Shanti Project, the organization I was introduced to shortly after Amanda died. The trainer told us the story of a taxi driver who was working the night shift in the city and took a call at 2:30 in the morning from a woman at a small apartment complex in a quiet part of town. When he arrived, the building was dark except for one light on the ground floor, and there was no response to his honk. Most drivers would have driven away, but this

> *"Love only grows by sharing. You can only have more for yourself by giving it away to others."*
> —Brian Tracy,
> *Maximum Achievement*

126

kind man was concerned that maybe the woman needed help, so he went to the door and knocked. After a few moments, an elderly woman opened the door, carrying a small suitcase. Behind her, the apartment looked abandoned, all the furniture covered with sheets.

It turned out this woman was going to the hospice to die, alone. She had no family left and the doctors had told her she didn't have very long to live. She asked him to drive her through downtown for the last time. Knowing that this was her final ride, he switched off the meter and told her he would drive her wherever she wanted to go for no charge.

She directed him around the city for the next couple of hours, showing him where she used to work, where she met her husband, where they went dancing, where they used to live. She told him stories from her life as they drove through the darkened streets. When he finally dropped her off at the hospice, as the sun was rising, they hugged, and she thanked him for giving an old woman a little moment of joy. Driving away, he kept asking himself, "What if that woman had gotten another driver, one who was angry or impatient? What if that other driver had just honked once, then driven away?" He felt filled with purpose and gratitude, reflecting afterward that it might have been the most important thing he ever did in his life.

I was so moved when I heard that story, because it captures, for me, the essence of what it means to be a giver. It means making yourself available for moments like that. How many opportunities do you miss every day to make that kind of difference? It might take as little as a smile or a kind gesture to change another person's day, or even to change someone's life.

I recently discovered the work of a guy who's actually come up with a job description that encompasses this attitude. His business cards say "David Wagner: Daymaker." Wagner is a hairdresser by profession, but his real calling is a life of service through small but powerful acts of kindness. In his book *Life as a Daymaker*, he describes how he came to the realization that his purpose in life was to "make people's days." It began, for him, when one of his regular clients came in to have her hair styled a couple weeks before her usual appointment. He figured she must have an important social engagement, but when he inquired about her plans, she said she just wanted to look and feel good that night. Wagner gave her special attention, massaging her scalp and joking and laughing with her as he styled her hair. When she left, she smiled radiantly and hugged him goodbye. He writes:

> *"A few days later, when I received a letter from this client, I began to realize the enormous potential of Daymaking. My client admitted that she had wanted her hair styled so it would look good for her funeral. She had planned to commit suicide later that day. But the wonderful time she had during our appointment had given her hope that things could get better. She decided to check herself into the hospital and get professional help. She thanked me for caring, even though I didn't know what she was going through."*36

Like the cab driver, Wagner immediately wondered how things might have turned out differently if he'd not been there for her. What if he had been distracted or hurried in his time with her? He resolved from then on to treat every person he met like that woman, and to train everyone who worked in his network of salons to do the same.

These two stories illustrate a powerful principle: we never know what impact our simple acts of kindness and availability can have. As you go through your daily life, experiment with giving just a little more of your attention to the people you interact with. Leave aside your own thoughts, worries, or frustrations for a minute as you interact with the checkout person at the grocery store, for a half hour as you meet with a client or colleague, or for the space of a meal shared with family or friends. Notice how much of the time you are distracted and not fully present. Take a risk to leave all those nagging thoughts aside for now. Don't worry—if they're important, they'll still be there when you are done giving your attention to someone else.

Peer Support: The Shanti Model

I first heard the taxi driver story above when I participated in volunteer training at the Shanti Project, the organization that I became connected with after Amanda's passing. Shanti has a unique way of working that resonates very deeply with my approach to life, which is why I'm so delighted that the Love From Margot Foundation will be partnering with them in their work.

Founded in 1974 by Dr. Charles Garfield, Shanti is dedicated to enhancing quality of life for people living with life-threatening or chronic illnesses by providing volunteer-based emotional and practical support. As described in the organization's mission statement, "Shanti is a Sanskrit word meaning 'inner peace' or 'tranquility.' It is an appropriate name since, ultimately, all of Shanti's direct service and educational programs are aimed at easing the burdens and improving the well-being of people in difficult life situations."

The model Shanti uses for its volunteer work is called the Shanti Model of Peer Support, described as "a way of being with another person that frees both parties to be fully who they are and communicate their feelings to one another. It is a way of being which allows two persons to meet as equals. It is a way of relating to others that is characterized by certain values and attitudes."

Shanti teaches its volunteers how to meet clients as equals, meaning that they are to create an environment of mutual respect, authenticity, acceptance, and empathy. The organization emphasizes that the volunteers should not assume a position of authority. Rather, they should "assume that the client has solutions to his or her own problems and does not need your advice or direction." Volunteers should come with the simple intention to be present and be of service.

Having spoken to volunteers at Shanti, and subsequently having gone through the training myself, I can attest to the power of this approach. Much of it comes down to the ability to listen—to give another person your full and undivided attention, free from agendas, judgments, or positions. Not only does it profoundly ease the final days and weeks of the clients Shanti serves, but over and over again I hear stories of how it has also transformed the lives of the volunteers, who have discovered the power of giving.

You can learn more about the work of the Shanti Project at www.shanti.org. Perhaps you will even be inspired to volunteer!

You Can't Out-Give God

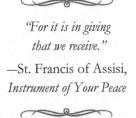

If you start giving—be it money, time, work, or simply love, availability, and attention—you may notice a surprising result. I spoke earlier about the sense that something

"For it is in giving that we receive."

—St. Francis of Assisi, *Instrument of Your Peace*

is missing, the inner void that we feel we need to fill. When you turn that notion on its head and start giving instead of taking, you will find, to your surprise, that you start filling up. This is sometimes called "the law of reciprocity," and I believe it's as much a part of how our universe works as the law of gravity. It simply states that what you freely give with a loving heart comes back to you, multiplied.

This sentiment is expressed beautifully by many of the greatest spiritual and motivational teachers I've been inspired by, starting with Zig Ziglar, whose seminar I attended back in 1980 when I felt like my life couldn't get much worse. I remember him saying, "You can have everything you want in life if you help enough other people get what they want." The same basic idea can be found in many places in the Bible. "Give and it will be given to you," says Luke (6:38). I like this version of the message from Corinthians 9:6-8

> *Whoever sows generously will also reap generously. Each man should give what he has decided in his heart to give, not reluctantly or under compulsion, for God loves a cheerful giver. And God is able to make all grace abound to you, so that in all things at all times, having all that you need, you will abound in every good work*

Another way I've heard it put is, "You can't out-give God." If you're not comfortable with that term, substitute "the universe" instead—the principle remains the same. No matter how much you give, more will come back to you. The only caveat is that you have to give with a pure heart, out of love—not out of duty, obligation, or desire for anything in return.

Since I sat by Amanda's deathbed and received the extraordinary gift of purpose, the truth of the law of reciprocity has amazed me. My mother taught me this as a child, but I got lost in self-centeredness for much of my life and forgot about it. Now I experience an unquenchable desire to help others and share whatever love and support I am able to provide. I've noticed that as soon as this momentum of giving was set in motion within my heart, magic began happening in my life on a daily basis. The right people started to appear just when I needed them, resources became abundant, and situations that would once have been difficult to navigate began to flow effortlessly. It really did seem as if the stars had begun to align.

The purpose of life is to serve. Don't wait to start giving until you feel you have enough or are good enough. Start today, right now, with an open and compassionate heart. Give love, give kindness, give a smile, or simply give your attention. It will come back to you one hundredfold.

Living in Balance

66 "I f your compassion does not include yourself, it is incomplete,"[37] writes meditation teacher Jack Kornfield. This is an important and sometimes difficult lesson to learn as we explore how to live a life of love and service. In order to be of service to the world, you have to be of service to yourself. In order to care for others, you have to care for yourself. If you are living an unbalanced, stress-filled, miserable life, you will be limited in how much energy and love you can give.

"The ingredients of both darkness and light are equally present in all of us . . .the madness of this world is largely a result of the human being's difficulty in coming to virtuous balance with himself."
—Elizabeth Gilbert,
Eat, Pray, Love

What I have learned, in my own journey, is that the key to having love and compassion for oneself is to find *balance*. Creating balance in your own life allows you to have a strong and stable foundation from which to give freely.

Balance has not come naturally to me, to put it mildly. I have always been a person of extremes. I would either drink like a fish or be a teetotaler. I went from being completely broke to being abundantly wealthy. I'm not inclined to do anything in moderation. I guess I may have inherited this tendency from my father, who came from a terrible childhood to become a professional baseball player for a couple of years before dropping out of the sport to marry my mom and become the youngest national sales manager in Proctor & Gamble's history—and eventually became a hard core alcoholic. (I am proud to say that after many years of complete and utter destruction, Dad currently has over thirty years of sobriety and has helped a large number of people to obtain the same.) My memories of childhood are of moving between two completely different worlds—the one when my father was away on his frequent sales trips and the one when he was home

When Dad was gone, life in our house was full of fun, laughter, and board games, with dinner on the table at six and my mom happy, loving, and attentive. When he was home, dinner was rarely on the table before eight. He would get home at six, and Mom's attention would be immediately on him. They would drink for a few hours, which would give rise sometimes to great humor and frivolity and other times to angry outbursts. My childhood oscillated on a weekly basis between normalcy and chaos, which may explain why, as

"Happiness is not a matter of intensity but of balance and order and rhythm and harmony."
—Thomas Merton,
No Man is an Island

I moved into adult life, I had a tendency to create chaos whenever things got too good. It's taken me many years to fully appreciate what it means to be in balance—spiritually, physically, mentally, and emotionally.

What Is Balance?

The word "balance" can be interpreted in many different ways. I focus on balancing four main areas of my life: body, mind, heart, and soul. I have found that if I can create balance in these four "macro" dimensions, the other parts of life start to line up and take care of themselves.

It's important to give attention to all four: body, mind, heart, and soul. I have noticed that many contemporary teachers and coaches tend to focus on three: mind, body, and spirit. Too often, they neglect the heart, which is an essential piece of what it means to live a balanced life. When I talk about the heart, of course, I am not talking about the physical organ but about the dimension of our lives where we experience emotions, where we give and receive love, where we feel pain and joy and compassion. To live a life of joy and service, we must balance and nourish our body, mind, heart, and soul. Just as we feed our mind with knowledge, we feed our soul with contemplation and silence. Just as we nourish our body with wholesome foods, we must nourish our heart through practicing kindness and compassion.

Think of these as being like the four wheels on a carriage. If one of the wheels is smaller, damaged, or out of shape, the carriage won't be able to roll smoothly down the road. It will be off-balance and in danger of tipping over. If each wheel is equally sized and equally well cared for, however, the carriage will roll smoothly and be able to gain momentum, making it easier to travel down the road. In the same way, when you are out of · balance in your life, you are much more likely to make mistakes or choices that you will one day regret. And you will use up much of your precious energy trying to stay on track, compensating for the imbalance.

When you're in balance, your energy and attention will no longer be absorbed in this way and you will start to feel a natural momentum carrying you forward. The motivational speaker Brian Tracy uses a similar metaphor: "Just as your car runs more smoothly and requires less energy to go faster and farther when the wheels are in perfect alignment, you perform better when your thoughts, feelings, emotions, goals, and values are in balance."[38]

Let's look a little closer at what it means to take care of each of the four dimensions of being human: heart, mind, body, and soul. We will start with the heart, as it is the most often neglected.

Taking Care of the Heart

Until I was in my early twenties, I couldn't even define emotions. Of course, I had them and I reacted out of them, but I didn't really understand the concept of emotion. I couldn't name

"It is only with the heart that one can see rightly; what is essential is invisible to the eye."

—Antoine de Saint Exupéry, *The Little Prince*

what I was feeling. I later learned that this is not so unusual—researchers studying "emotional intelligence" have found that the maturing of our capacities for emotional self-awareness, empathy, and emotional self-management are dependent on the full development of the prefrontal cortex in the brain, which typically does not occur until somewhere between the ages of twenty-two and twenty-five.

Taking care of the heart starts with the ability to be aware of your own emotions, which is a prerequisite for being able to empathize with the emotions of another person. When you feel emotions arising, practice simply naming them. Do this without judgment—remember, as we discussed in Chapter 2, that the willingness to embrace and accept our own "shadow," including all the emotions we don't like or are ashamed of, is essential. If you are unable to accept the full range of your emotional experience, you will repress aspects of yourself, creating a lack of balance and integration.

Once you begin to be intimate with your emotional life, you can move to a deeper level of nourishing the heart. The beauty of this dimension of self is that it is nourished not through consumption but through expression. While the body and the mind are nourished by what they take in, the heart is nourished by what it gives.

The Buddhists have a beautiful Sanskrit word, *metta*, which means "loving-kindness." One of the central practices in many schools of Buddhism is a meditation on loving-kindness. As is written in the *Dhammapada*, a collection of the sayings of the Buddha, "Animosity does not eradicate animosity. Only by loving-kindness is animosity dissolved."[39]

You don't have to be a Buddhist to practice this kind of meditation. Just close your eyes and visualize a field of loving-kindness expanding out from your heart. First, focus that loving-kindness on yourself. Then think of a friend or loved one and focus the loving-kindness upon him or her. Then direct your loving-kindness toward a stranger, someone you feel neither positive nor negative about. Next, visualize someone you are in conflict with—someone you dislike or resent. Focus your loving-kindness on that person. Finally, allow the field of loving-kindness to expand to all sentient beings.

In the Tibetan Buddhist tradition, there is a similar practice known as *tonglen*. In this kind of meditation, you focus on your breathing. With each exhalation, you imagine sending happiness out into the world, and with each inhalation, you receive and absorb suffering.

Try these exercises, or simply practice giving in one of the many ways we discussed in the previous chapter. The way to take care of your heart is to be loving, open, and compassionate in as many interactions as possible on a daily basis.

Taking Care of the Body

My New Year's resolution the year Margot lay dying was easy: No more activities that waste time or energy, and no more choices that endanger my

"To keep the body in good health is a duty, for otherwise we shall not be able to trim the lamp of wisdom, and keep our mind strong and clear."

—Gautama Buddha, *The Sermon at Benares*

body. I had seen firsthand the preciousness of health and life. The most powerful lesson of Margot's illness and her death was that love—the essence of who we are—is not limited or bound by the physical body. But I also learned to treasure the body as the vehicle through which love can live and act in this world. The body, the ancient wisdom traditions tell us, is the temple of the spirit. Therefore, to care for the body is to care for the spirit.

Jesus said that we are "in the world but not of the world." I believe that who we are, at the most essential level, transcends the physical dimension. But our bodies are "of this world," and as long as we are living here on this earth, we are trapped within these extraordinary but fragile organisms made up of sixty to eighty trillion cells. The more we take care of those trillions of cells, the more available we will be to live, and love, and give.

According to the principles of Maslow's Hierarchy of Needs, which we discussed in Chapter 1, if you are not taking care of the needs of your body, your attention will not be free to even become aware of the needs of the other dimensions of your being—of your mind, your heart, or your soul—let alone the needs of others.

I am not a medical doctor (although I've spent a large part of my life in hospitals and have read countless books on the subject of health), so it is not my place to offer specific advice or direction on health or nutrition. But I will say that from personal experience, I am firmly convinced that one of the most powerful things we can do to take care of our bodies is to increase the amount of life-giving oxygen we feed to our cells. Most of us never think about how we are breathing. But as an ancient

Sanskrit proverb says, "Breath is life, and if you breathe well you will live long on Earth."

Our breath is the essence of life—the first thing we do when we are born and the last thing we do before we die. In many languages, the word for breath and the word for spirit are the same. When the breath leaves the body, the spirit is gone.

Paying attention to your breathing and learning to breathe more deeply means that you are carrying more oxygen to your bloodstream. This can be achieved through yoga or meditative practices that teach you to focus on your breath. It can also be achieved through aerobic exercise, which has many other benefits as well.

The other key element of taking care of the body is, of course, how we nourish ourselves. The common saying "you are what you eat" is all too true—we only have to look at our fast-food-loving, overweight, unhealthy American culture to see the evidence. I am not trying to pass judgment on anyone for particular lifestyle choices or pretend to be an authority in this regard. I imagine that many of my readers may know more about this dimension of life than I do. However, if this is an area that you struggle with, or if you know you have unhealthy eating habits, I will simply say that if you start eating fresh, nutritious, unprocessed organic food, and avoid chemically processed foods and excessive sugar, you will notice the effects on your body and mind very quickly. You will start to feel vibrant, energetic, and awake. Your consciousness will feel clearer, as if a fog of dullness and fatigue has cleared. And most importantly, you will be more available to give.

Health is foundational to everything else you do. You could have the mind of Einstein, the heart of Mother Teresa, and the spirit of Christ, but if you don't have enough physical energy to get off the couch, what is the purpose of living? What good can you do in the world, for yourself or for your family?

If you have your health, you are rich. Your job may be tough, your finances may be low, you may suffer emotionally in various ways, but you have a gift that you should never take for granted. If you have, as I did, watched someone you love suffer beyond comprehension as their body succumbs to disease, you will no doubt be grateful every day for the blessing of good health. And you will be inspired to take the best care you possibly can of your particular trillions of cells.

Taking Care of the Mind

Mental health is a term we tend to use with regard to people who have mental illnesses. We don't think of it as something that all of us should be working on in our daily lives. But in fact, our minds are the source of much of our suffering, and we can have a tremendous impact on our quality of life by learning how to cultivate a healthy mind.

"When the mind is kept away from its preoccupations, it becomes quiet. If you do not disturb this quiet and stay in it, you will find it is permeated with a light and a love you have never known."

—Nisargadatta Maharaj,
I Am That

In my experience, there are two fundamental components to taking care of the mind:

1. Gaining greater control over the mind.
2. Letting go of the mind.

I learned about taking control of the mind back in my early twenties when I first heard Zig Ziglar speak, and later when I began to work with John the mystery man. Both of them, along with most of the great personal-development teachers, point out that what is in our minds has a profound effect on who we are and what our lives look like. I remember Ziglar, in that first seminar, declaring, "You're where you are, you're what you are, because of what has gone into your mind." He loved to say, "Garbage in, garbage out!"

Taking care of the mind, in this sense, means bringing greater awareness to what is going into your mind. In our media-saturated culture, it's so easy to allow our minds to be flooded with negative images, messages, and ideas. If we don't put up any filters and just absorb it all, it's no wonder that the output is often not positive.

A key to mental health, then, is to realize that you can control what you listen to, what you watch, and what you expose yourself to. I make a conscious choice not to watch television or listen to certain radio stations, only getting my news from a few trusted, balanced sources. Try this for a week and see how it impacts your life. Make a conscious effort to surround yourself with positive people and positive messages, and to engage in a positive outlook. If there are people in your life who drag you down, berate you, or do nothing to support or uplift you, it is important to first appreciate their role in your life and then take the bold step to leave them behind.

The second element of mental health is learning to question and let go of your thoughts. This is what I learned when I studied with Byron Katie, and it is a central tenet of many of the mystical traditions. They point out to us that we are unquestioningly identified with our minds, with our stories. We think that our thoughts are who we are, and this causes us to suffer.

Many of the different forms of meditation are variations on the theme of questioning or letting go of the endlessly chattering thought stream—what the Buddhists call the "monkey mind." People often think that the idea of meditation is to quiet the mind completely. If you've tried this, you'll realize that it's easier said than done, to say the least. But others point out that a completely quiet mind is not necessarily the goal. A more helpful way to think about meditation, they teach us, is to see it as a way to create space between yourself and your thoughts, and in doing so, to question your identification with the mind.

For me, the first powerful experience of this came when Byron Katie taught me to question my story, as I shared in Chapter 5. The second came when I read about the great Indian saint Ramana Maharshi, who died in 1950. One of the most revered spiritual figures of modern India, Maharshi came to his spiritual awakening through asking the question, "Who am I?" in such a way that he penetrated through all the layers of thought to discover the deeper self that lay beyond the mind. In his book *Be As You Are: The Teachings of Ramana Maharshi,*

David Godman records Maharshi's instructions for this practice, known as "self-inquiry":

> *At the very moment that each thought rises, if one vigilantly enquires "To whom did this rise?," it will be known "To me." If one then enquires "Who am I?," the mind will turn back to its source [the Self] and the thought which had risen will also subside. By repeatedly practicing thus, the power of the mind to abide in its source increases.*40

I have found this practice to be tremendously helpful when I'm tied up in knots with my mind. If I'm in a tough spot, a moment of anxiety, confusion, or fear, I'll ask myself the question, "Who am I?" and everything softens. What arises is a recognition of who I am not: I am not my body, I am not my problems, I am not my thoughts. I am far greater. I am a timeless eternal soul with unlimited potential—that is who I really am.

There are many other forms of meditation, depending on your preferences. Some use a repeated phrase, or *mantra*, to focus their attention away from thought. Others use the breath. If nothing else, simply try sitting still and quiet for a period of time each day, observing the movement of thought.

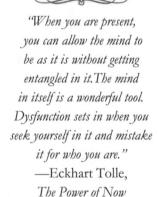

"When you are present, you can allow the mind to be as it is without getting entangled in it. The mind in itself is a wonderful tool. Dysfunction sets in when you seek yourself in it and mistake it for who you are."
—Eckhart Tolle,
The Power of Now

Taking Care of the Soul

I recently put my home on the market, and so I prepared it for an open house, where prospective buyers could look around. Before people arrived, I took a walk around the house myself, trying to look at it as if I were a stranger. When I came to my bookshelf, I was struck by the range of titles that shared one shelf. Besides numerous self-help books, there were several Bibles; books by contemporary spiritual teachers like Eckhart Tolle, Byron Katie, and Ram Dass; books on Buddhism; Hindu texts; and a copy of the Koran. What would people make of this? I wondered. What would they conclude about someone who reads all this?

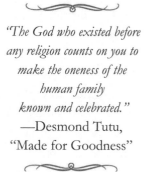

"The God who existed before any religion counts on you to make the oneness of the human family known and celebrated."
—Desmond Tutu, "Made for Goodness"

My bookshelf is a reflection of how I take care of my soul. All my life, I have been fascinated by religion and spirituality, by life and death, by the fundamental question, "Why are we here?" I guess you could say I am a seeker of truth, which, as I understand it, is always evolving. I grew up Catholic, and Margot and I attended Mass every Sunday while she was sick. For a period in my life, before I met Margot, I was a born-again Christian. These days, I don't belong to any particular denomination, but I practice elements of both Christianity and Buddhism.

At this point in my life, based on everything I've learned, I have certain beliefs, and the most fundamental one is that we are all connected. I believe that at the heart of all manmade religions is this same message. I hear a fundamental unity of wisdom beneath their different myths, methods, and mysteries. They tell us that God is love, they tell us to serve others, and they tell us that we are all one. As the great religious scholar Aldous Huxley wrote in the 1940s, in his seminal book *The Perennial Philosophy*, there is a central truth to all the great traditions, a single message that is merely garbed in different clothing according to tradition and culture. Huxley claimed that all the religious traditions point to "the more or less obscure intuition of the oneness that is the ground and principle of all multiplicity."[41] In other words, they tell us that beneath the appearance of many, there is one. Whatever different names they give that One, all the religions describe it. Margot believed this too, writing toward the end of her life, "I choose to believe that all of us are connected by an invisible power/energy. This power goes by many names, but I choose to call it God."

You do not have to be religious to believe that we are all connected. Even scientists are now demonstrating the many ways in which we are interdependent and interconnected—from ecologists to quantum physicists. Albert Einstein wrote in a letter to a grieving friend that, "A human being is part of a whole, called by us 'Universe,' a part limited in time and space. He experiences himself, his thoughts and feelings, as something separated from the rest—a kind of optical delusion of his consciousness. The striving to free oneself from this delusion is the one issue of true religion."[42]

I think it's important that we make a distinction between spirituality and religion. This is not to say one is better than the other. I have been religious much of my life, but I have learned that being spiritual does not depend on believing in the tenets of any religion. To me, spirituality is the belief in the fundamental oneness that is the source of all religions, which is why I have books from such a wide variety of faiths on my bookshelf. If you are not religious at all, you can still be spiritual. And if you are a practitioner of a particular faith, you can find spirituality through your tradition.

Taking care of your soul may take many forms, depending on your particular beliefs. But in essence, it means taking time to remind yourself that we are all one. Whether you do this through prayer, through contemplation, through spending time in nature, or through any other means, make time to do it, every day.

Persevering Through Difficult Times

"Life is difficult." I will never forget these opening words of M. Scott Peck's *The Road Less Traveled.*[43] When I read them for the first time, I

> *"If you are going through hell, keep going."*
> —Winston Churchill

realized that I, like many people in the West, had a deeply held belief that life should be easy. As we explore the topic of balance, it is important to reflect on this belief. Balance does not mean that we will be able to miraculously avoid the challenges of life. But it may

149

mean that we can navigate them more gracefully, just as a carriage with four good wheels is more likely to stay upright when it hits a bump or a pothole.

A key part of balance, I have learned, is accepting the good and the bad, the light and the dark. None of us wants to suffer, but sometimes suffering is a great teacher. Margot knew this long before I did. A few months before she died, she wrote in a message to my daughter, "I have traveled and seen pain and watched the humanity of despair. Dad [me] doesn't know this yet, but sometimes suffering brings you closer to God, closer to what it means to be human. . . . Pain is an enlightenment, but only if you see it that way." I find it interesting that Margot said "yet," as if she knew that one day I would learn this lesson. She was right. Since she died, I have learned this truth. I no longer seek to run away from the difficulties of challenges, and I find greater balance and groundedness in embracing reality, however it presents itself.

The Importance of Being Truthful

A final key to living a life of balance is the simple but powerful practice of truthfulness. As Don Miguel Ruiz puts it in *The Four Agreements,* "Be impeccable with your word." There is nothing that will throw you off balance faster than an untruth or even a half-truth, a lack of integrity, or a failure to be consistent and transparent in your actions. Mark Twain is said to have joked that, "If you tell the truth, you don't have to remember anything," but his humorous remark is worth taking seriously. Think about how quickly your mind gets

"Be impeccable with your word. Speak with integrity. Say only what you mean. Avoid using the word to speak against yourself or to gossip about others. Use the power of your word in the direction of truth and love."

—Don Miguel Ruiz,
The Four Agreements

preoccupied when you have something to hide. Being impeccable with your word frees you from this preoccupation.

I read Don Miguel's book prior to my nine-day course with Byron Katie, shortly after Margot's death. I hadn't fully appreciated his teaching before then, but as I watched Katie for nine days, listening to her every word and watching her every action, I observed that she was impeccable with her word like no one else I had ever known. Don Miguel's teaching fully resonated deep within me as I watched a living example.

Practices for Balance

"Next to love, balance is the most important thing."

—Coach John Wooden

Take an Inventory

As you start to engage with this idea of balance, it can be helpful to take stock of where you are, where you have come from, and where you are going.

Pick a point about five years ago, and try to take yourself back to how you felt at that moment in your life. Examine each area of life: your physical health and vitality (body), your mental clarity and freedom (mind), your emotional well-being and generosity (heart), and your sense of spiritual connection (soul). Give yourself a score from one to ten for each dimension, and write a few words or sentences to describe your state of body, mind, heart, and soul. Now repeat the same exercise for the present moment. Compare the scores and descriptions, and ask yourself first if you have developed in each area. Are you going forward or backward? And second, ask yourself if there is a balance between the four. Which areas are more developed than others? Finally, project yourself five years into the future, and imagine what it would look like for you to get a higher score in each area *and* to bring all four to the same level. Once you have completed this exercise, ask yourself what steps you could take today to move yourself forward toward balance. Identify one simple concrete step for each of the four dimensions, and practice it each day.

"A life worth living is worth recording."
—Tony Robbins

Keep a Journal

One practice that nourishes heart, mind, and soul is the practice of keeping a journal. For most of my life I have kept a journal, and I value having a record of my life that I can periodically look back over, reflecting on the things that I struggled with and overcame, and on my many blessings. I try to take a quiet time every morning to write in my journal. My approach is very simple. It has three steps, beginning with gratitude and ending with love.

    1. **Gratitude.** I start by thanking God or the universe for all the things in my life that I am

grateful for. Gratitude opens the heart and connects you to the energy of love and abundance.

2. **Ask for Wisdom.** I believe that there is a field of energy and intelligence in the universe that can help me to find guidance in my life. I ask for wisdom in navigating whatever choices, challenges, or dilemmas are facing me. Writing down each specific situation helps to invite the wisdom in and focus the energy of the universe on that particular issue.

3. **Love.** I end with offering thanks and love to the power and energy that connects us all.

Here is an example of one of my journal entries from 2007. As you will see, I asked for wisdom on very practical matters that I was struggling with. I address my journal entries to "Heavenly Father," as this resonates with my faith, but you can also address them to the universe or whatever name or symbol represents a greater wisdom than yourself.

Dear Heavenly Father, thank you for this day. Thank you for my wife, my children, and my family. Thank you for this country that I live in and the freedom that I enjoy. Thank you for my health. Thank you for my business.

Father, I pray for the following:

  1. That Margot will be healed from her illness.

153

2. *That Kelli will find the things that will motivate her to go in a positive direction.*
3. *That Michelle will have an easy and successful pregnancy.*
4. *That my father will find peace in the midst of his mourning.*

Lord, I ask for wisdom on the following:

1. *What to do with the Tahoe house.*
2. *How to help Margot with her diet and exercise plans.*
3. *Whether or not to buy the building next to Broadway VW and expand the business.*
4. *How to get through to Kelli.*
5. *How to lose 15 pounds and be healthier.*

Thank you, Lord. I love you.

Some days my entries are short; some days they are long. I spend about ten minutes each day journaling, followed by about five minutes just sitting and being quiet. I hope that you will try it. You will be amazed, years later, when you look back and see the miracles that have happened as a result of writing down your desires!

If you can learn to balance body, mind, heart, and soul, you will find yourself available to contribute in a way that may astonish you. Imagine living a life where you jump out of bed at first light, filled with energy you haven't had since you were five years old. Imagine being able to begin the day with time for reflection, before throwing yourself into your work, giving fully to doing what you love, taking care of your body, and then falling peacefully asleep, before waking up revitalized, ready to do it all over again. Imagine feeling both deep peace and energizing purpose, grounding you and propelling you forward, from one day to the next, from one week to the next, from one year to the next. That is what balancing body, mind, heart, and soul makes possible.

You Are Small . . . But You Are Infinite

Some nights, I love to sit out in front of my house, as a gentle breeze blows down off the slopes of Mount Diablo, and contemplate the stars. When we are seeking purpose and balance in life, and trying to figure out what we are here to contribute, there is a lot to be learned from what science has shown us about the extraordinary cosmos we are part of. Here are some of the things I call to mind when I'm in need of a little perspective.

According to astronomers, our galaxy, the Milky Way, contains up to 400 billion stars and planets of various sizes and brightness. And since the Hubble telescope has allowed scientists to see so much more of the cosmos, they now estimate that there are hundreds of billions of other

"Our deepest fear is not that we are inadequate. Our deepest fear is that we are powerful beyond measure. It is our light, not our darkness that most frightens us."

—Marianne Williamson, *A Return to Love*

galaxies out there, of which our Milky Way, about 100,000 to 120,000 light years in diameter, is just one average-sized example. When I'm feeling overwhelmed by personal problems or by the challenges of my particular day-to-day existence, just reminding myself how vast the cosmos is can help to put things in perspective. In light of that immensity, who am I to make too much of a big deal about myself? As the great cosmologist Carl Sagan put it, "Who are we? We find that we live on an insignificant planet of a humdrum star lost in a galaxy tucked away in some forgotten corner of a universe in which there are far more galaxies than people."[44]

After stretching my mind to try and encompass the immeasurable scale of the universe, I come slowly back to myself, one step at a time. Our galaxy is one within hundreds of billions. Our sun is just one star out of as many as 400 billion in its own galaxy, and our planet is just one of the many orbiting that sun. On our planet, there are more than 7 billion human beings, each with a particular story to tell. I am just one of those 7 billion, living in North America, in the state of California, born into my particular family, and living out my life's story. By the time I get all the way back to my body, sitting there on my deck gazing upward, I feel like I'm just a speck of dust in the cosmic landscape.

The amazing thing about looking at the stars is that we're not just looking out into the vastness of space— we're also looking back into the vastness of time. The light that reaches our perception has traveled across billions of years. Cosmologists tell us that the universe has been expanding and developing for 13.7 billion years—a stretch of time so immense that the human mind cannot even begin to imagine it. About 13 billion years ago, clouds of atoms began to collapse into the primal galaxies, and by 12 billion years ago, our Milky Way came into being, along with some hundred billion other galaxies. Our sun was born about 4.5 billion years ago, followed a few million years later by our beautiful blue-green planet, with its unusually life-friendly conditions. In some "warm little pond," as Darwin speculated, the first cells appeared around 4 billion years ago, and began the slow and miraculous journey of life, from single cells to multi-celled organisms to all the diversity of plants and insects and birds and animals and finally—200,000 years ago—to us. "Human consciousness arose but a minute before midnight on the geological clock," writes scientist Stephen Jay Gould, comparing us, in the context of evolutionary history, to mayflies, which live just a few hours on a spring day.[45]

When we realize how miniscule we are and how brief our lifespans, within this infinitely large universe and its infinitely long history, there are several ways that can impact our perspective. I've seen people respond to this picture in two dramatically different ways.

The first response is to conclude that because we are so small, we are bound to be insignificant. What purpose or meaning could there be to the actions and choices of a speck of dust? What difference could this tiny, brief life actually make? If we conclude this, it is logical that we would dedicate the brief time we have to trying to get as much as we can for ourselves, attempting to make our short lives as comfortable and as pleasurable as possible. This fits in nicely with the message we get from the media and corporate advertising: that the only purpose in life is to get the biggest house, the nicest car, the most stylish clothes, the most attractive partner, and so on. We try to fill the void of insignificance with possessions and short-term entertainment.

If you've read this far in the book, it won't come as a surprise to you that this is not the conclusion I draw. When I look at the stars and think about how small I am and how brief my lifetime is, it certainly helps me not to take my own story—with its drama and struggle and victories and joys—too seriously. But it doesn't leave me feeling purposeless. In fact, quite the opposite. I think this is because I don't feel distant or disconnected from that vast cosmos. I remember reading about how the very atoms that make up our bodies were forged in the fiery hearts of stars that died long before our sun was born. "The history of the universe is in every one of us," write Joel Primack and Nancy Abrams in *The View from the Center of the Universe*. "Every particle in our bodies has a multibillion-year past, every cell and every bodily organ has a multimillion-year past." [46] The stars are our birthplace. We are, as Sagan said, "star-stuff contemplating the stars."[47] Therefore, when I look up at the stars, I know that I am seeing, as some cosmologists poetically put it, my ancestors. And while I feel small, I also feel infinite, expanded by the knowledge that I am connected to the vastness of this universe.

An Interconnected Whole

As I have shared in these chapters, I believe that everything is interconnected, and that there is an energy field that binds it all—from the most distant stars to the web of life on our particular planet, to you and I and our network of relationships. This energy is the energy of love. There may be billions of us, on one small star among

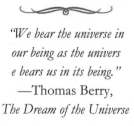

"We bear the universe in our being as the univers e bears us in its being."
—Thomas Berry,
The Dream of the Universe

billions of stars, but we are connected. We are all one. Think about an ocean: it contains countless billions of molecules of water. Any one of those molecules, alone, would be insignificant and powerless. But those water molecules are much more powerful, fluid, and living when bound together to form an ocean. The universal energy of love is the binding agent that pervades and invades the inner essence of all of us.

If you can get even an inkling of your oneness with everything in the cosmos, you will realize the beautiful paradox that although you are small, you are also infinite. Pierre Teilhard de Chardin, a great French mystical thinker from the early twentieth century, who was also a paleontologist, described this paradox when he wrote, "At once humbled and ennobled by our discoveries, we are gradually coming to see ourselves as a part of vast and continuing processes; as though awakening from a dream, we are beginning to realize that our nobility consists in serving, like intelligent atoms, the work proceeding in the Universe. We have discovered that there is a Whole, of which we are the elements. We have found the world in our own souls."[48]

A common deterrent to those of us who feel called to serve, to live for a higher purpose, is the feeling that we are small and insignificant and could not possibly make a difference to the large, complicated, and innumerable problems in the world. But the metaphor of atoms is a helpful one. Imagine if the atoms in your body felt that they were too insignificant to have any function, and decided to stop combining into molecules. Imagine if your cells decided that they were too small to matter, and stopped cooperating with each other to form your organs, your blood, your skin, or your muscles. Each of us is like an atom in the great process of life, or like a cell in the larger body of humanity. We cannot know what our impact will be, but because we are connected to everything, it may be much greater than you realize. The great naturalist John Muir described this beautifully when he wrote, "When we try to pick out anything by itself we find that it is bound fast by a thousand invisible cords that cannot be broken, to everything in the universe."[49] Respond to the problems that present themselves in front of you, to the people or situations that need your help. You don't know how far the effects will be felt through those invisible cords.

I believe our potential for greatness is unlocked when we realize we are one. When we stop believing the narrative society has told us—that we are separate, insignificant, and purposeless—and realize that we are all one, we cannot help but love one another with empathy and compassion. And every act of compassion ripples out through the field of energy that connects us, like a pebble thrown in the ocean ripples out through countless drops of water.

Making a Difference

There is a beautiful parable that illustrates this principle. I don't know who originally wrote the story, but I have heard it retold many times. It tells of an old man who was walking along a deserted beach at sunset. As he walked, he could see a young boy in the distance. Drawing nearer, he noticed that the boy kept bending down, picking something up, and throwing it into the water. Over and over again, the boy repeated the same motion, hurling things into the ocean. As the man approached the boy, he was able to see what the boy was picking up: starfish that had been washed up on the beach and left on the sand by the receding tide. One at a time, he was throwing them back into the water.

When the man asked the boy why he was doing this, the boy replied, "I am throwing these washed-up starfish back into the ocean, or else they will die from dehydration."

The man shook his head. "There are thousands of starfish on this beach. You can't possibly save them all. And this beach is just one of hundreds along the coast. You can't possibly make a difference."

The boy looked down, frowning for a moment, then bent to pick up another starfish, smiling as he threw it back into the sea. Turning to the old man, he replied, "I just made a huge difference to that one!"

This parable reminds us that every small act of love and compassion is making a world of difference to the recipient. And I believe it's also making a difference to the energy field that we are all connected by. At moments when I feel overwhelmed by the suffering in

163

the world, it helps me to remember to simply do what I can, one day at a time.

Margot's Starfish

As this book goes to press, the Love From Margot Foundation is nearing its two-year anniversary. Our "starfish" are mostly women from the San Francisco Bay Area where I have my offices and my car dealerships (which help me fund the foundation). In the past year, we have helped over thirty individuals with financial and medical assistance. In addition, through our partners— the Shanti Project in San Francisco, Highland Hospital in Oakland, and Gilda's Club in Palm Desert—we've helped hundreds more. Sometimes, when I think of all the people who are suffering from cancer and other terrible diseases, and all the people who don't have money or insurance to get good treatment, this seems like a tiny drop in the bucket. Am I really making a difference? But then I read their letters of thanks and realize what an enormous difference it has made to each individual. I don't really consider this "my" doing—it was Margot's love that opened my heart, and I feel as if it is still her love that flows through me and inspires me to help others. That is why the foundation is called Love From Margot. In the pages that follow, I will share some of the stories of the women we have helped, to demonstrate how one person's loving, open heart has touched so many other lives, even after she has passed from this world.

Amanda was our first client, and we were able to help pay for her and her family's lodging while she went through radiation treatment and for supplemental chemotherapy that Medicare would not pay for, giving her more time with her family. Here is what she wrote about the impact it had on her:

> *I was already flooded with bills from past treatments of Stage 4 breast cancer so now I was trying to penny pinch, so to speak, thinking of my loved ones and how hard it would be to pay off these bills if something were ever to happen to me. Margot's foundation gave me room to breathe. I did not have to ask how much is this or what is this going to cost or if they had something cheaper. Love From Margot Foundation has eased my mind. Stressing about financial issues just makes the pain worse and studies have shown that stress often enhances the process of cancer growth. I am now able to enjoy life more abundantly and not worry about penny pinching, I am now more assured that I am getting the best quality care and can still laugh and play with my children. Margot must have been an amazing woman, so compassionate about helping others; I wish I could give her a big hug and thank her for sending me love through this foundation.*

Beth applied to Love from Margot Foundation during the early summer of 2012 with Stage 2 breast cancer, aged 59. She writes:

> *I was diagnosed with Stage 2 breast cancer in December of 2011. I had recently lost my job due to budget cuts, so this was very difficult to deal with all at once. Of course, even though we hear the statistics, not one of us probably ever*

165

thought that it would be me. I know I didn't. As I stumbled through the maze of choices, decisions, information, resources, and trying to figure out what the best treatment plan for me was, all the while I also had to try to find some source of income. It isn't easy to search for employment knowing that you may not be able to make a commitment to the employer. After a lumpectomy, I decided that I would explore other options besides traditional chemotherapy and radiation. That's when they discovered another "mass" on my right ovary. After more surgery to remove the ovary, I was left weak but obviously very grateful that it was benign. I had received some financial help from my church, as well as a couple of well-known breast cancer foundations. Someone then told me about Love From Margot. I went to the website and knew immediately that this foundation was different. I could just feel the love pouring through the monitor screen! After I contacted them, I was amazed and relieved at the process and was deeply, deeply grateful that it seemed that someone on the other end of the line not only understood what I was going through, but expressed genuine compassion, understanding, and caring. I simply could not have survived this past year without this financial help. After I read the story of Margot, I was in tears and knew that I would do everything I could to help this organization. It's really the love that heals! I hope everyone reading this will donate whatever they can to help others regain their health, peace of mind, and ability to "pay it forward."

When I read words like this, I know without a doubt that Margot is still with me. Not only is she helping women like Beth fight their disease and pay their bills, but she is opening up their hearts in the same way she opened mine, so that they too feel inspired to serve.

Sandra applied to the Love from Margot Foundation in the late summer of 2012. She writes:

> *I was diagnosed with Stage 3 breast cancer on April 30, 2012. I was working two part-time jobs, had no health insurance, and was in the process of separating from my husband. I was not only in shock from the diagnosis but terrified of how I would take care of my children with the basics. I was placed on disability and earned $57 per week. My husband was helping as much as he could, but I did not have enough to take care of the monthly bills. I was told about the Love From Margot Foundation and found angels here on Earth. I requested a grant and was approved to receive a monthly amount. I can say the grant saved me and my children from losing our apartment, gave us electricity, helped with gas for school, and with my treatments. It also helped with the phone so that I could stay in communication with my children and my doctors. I am so grateful for the help the Love From Margot Foundation has provided. I could not have made it thus far without their aid. I cannot*

express the gratitude I feel. The ability to focus on my treatments and recovery is a tremendous blessing. I believe the stress relieved from the grant helped me to heal faster and stronger. I continue with treatment and look forward to the day I am in remission and able to return to work.

Malou came to us in the early fall of 2012 while undergoing treatment for Stage 2 breast cancer, which she had been battling for over a year. She had recently lost her job and was also taking care of her elderly mother. She writes:

I was born in the Democratic Republic of Congo and came to the United States in 1989. Since my arrival here, I have worked hard to make a life for myself, my mother, and my daughter. I always worked at least two jobs, so I could support and raise my daughter, since I was a single parent. In 2001, my mother came from the Congo to live with me; I have been her sole support since that time. For the past four years I have worked for Delta Airlines as a customer service representative and have had good health insurance. Unfortunately, in July of 2011, I was diagnosed with Stage 2 breast cancer. I had surgery, chemotherapy, and radiation treatments. This aggressive treatment has lasted over one year and I had to go on medical leave from work. I was emotionally, physically, and financially drained. I felt so hopeless and helpless during my treatments.

Because I was on leave from work, my health care premium increased from $65 a month to $650 a month for my Cobra payments. I was in despair, afraid that I would lose my insurance as I couldn't afford to pay for it with the money I got from State Disability.

If the Love from Margot Foundation had not stepped in, my insurance would have been canceled, I would not have been able to complete my treatment, and I would not have had a successful recovery. The Love from Margot Foundation is a great organization because it truly lives up to its name. It is an organization filled with love, warmth, kindness, and compassion. I am truly blessed to have encountered such a genuine and authentic organization that helped deliver me financially and gave me support in a time of darkness. I am forever grateful.

Malou has since returned to work and continues to be a dear friend and supporter of the foundation.

Stephanie learned about the Love from Margot Foundation from the poster board at my VW of Oakland dealership. She is a breast-cancer patient and mother of a pre-teen daughter. She lost her job on the first day she had radiation therapy and lost her insurance along with it. When she first came to us, she asked for any help she could get. "Maybe a Safeway card," she said. We are happy to have been able to help Stephanie with her expenses and were touched to receive a beautiful letter from her and her daughter thanking us for the money "on behalf of Margot's love and the love of those who loved her." She wrote, "Your support will help ease our burden a little and brighten our days as our small family fights this battle against breast cancer."

Margot's love lives on—in my heart, in the foundation, and in the lives of each of these women and the others we have helped, whether to pay a medical bill, save a home, pay for taxi rides, or buy a wig. It lives on in their children—some of whom still have a parent, and some of whom at least have a memory of a dignified, peaceful goodbye. It lives on in their grandchildren, like Amanda's baby granddaughter, for whom the foundation has set up a college fund. And it lives on in the small acts of kindness that each of those who are touched by our work are inspired to do themselves. We are each small, but together, we are infinite. Don't ever think your actions don't matter. Every starfish will thank you when you give it the gift of life.

Fulfilling the Promise

I began this book by sharing the story of a promise I had broken many decades ago, and the lack of fulfillment I was feeling in my life as a result. Since starting the Love From Margot Foundation, I have finally felt that sense of fulfillment and purpose flooding into each day. Most of our clients are living below the poverty line and battling life-threatening

"If you want others to be happy, practice compassion.
If you want to be happy, practice compassion."

—The Dalai Lama,
The Art of Happiness

diseases. I know Margot would have been so happy that we are able to help these people in her memory—she herself had grown up poor, in an immigrant family, and she was always rooting for the underdog.

My original promise, however, had been to help troubled youth like myself. And because our foundation's mission has room for me to make exceptions where I see fit, I have had the opportunity to come full circle and, at least in a few cases, fully make good on that original promise that I wrote down in the mystery man's kitchen: "to help teenagers and young adults who are neglected and struggling with their lives."

There have been a couple of cases where I've stepped outside our core mission to follow that original calling. Every person we help means the world to me, but these cases have had a particularly personal impact because of my own childhood experiences. My impulse to help troubled youth began long before I became one myself. The first stirrings of care in my heart began as a child when I heard my father's story of his own neglect by alcoholic parents and his time as a ward of the state. Later, that desire to help got muffled by my own exploits with drink, drugs, and crime, only to resurface briefly in my early twenties when I made the promise, before getting buried again beneath the surface comforts of a successful life.

The first kid I helped was the son of an old friend named Tim, who I'd grown up with in Cincinnati. We'd lost touch for many years but reconnected through a chance meeting at a baseball game in our hometown around the turn of the millennium. We both had kids, and his son Nick was the same age as my youngest daughter. We rekindled our friendship and had been close for more than a decade, playing golf together and visiting with each other's family, when Tim called me one day to say his son Nick had been arrested for heroin. He wanted to get Nick into a good rehab program, but his insurance

"Dare to reach out your hand into the darkness, to pull another hand into the light."

—Norman B. Rice, Commencement Speech at Whitmore College

wouldn't cover the full cost and his finances were tight.

I saw my chance to help a kid who was in worse shape than I had been in. Through a combination of foundation funds and my personal funds, I helped to pay for Nick's treatment. Feeling hopeful that he was on a better path, I turned my thoughts back to the foundation's mission. It would be some months before I heard from Nick's family again.

Saving Adam

The second kid I helped was even closer to home. When my kids were growing up, my son Christopher had a friend named Adam, who lived near our home in Danville, California. I remember Adam accompanying me, my kids, and Margot on a trip to Great America, a theme park in Santa Clara, when he must have been no more than twelve years old.

I loved the memories of that day, an oasis of fun and happiness right before the storm that would erupt when I left my wife and family. I kept a photograph of all the kids and me from that day at the park on my nightstand for years, so Adam's impish, freckled face was never far from my mind. A few years later, I heard he'd started to have problems with drugs. He took his first Vicodin in high school, at the age of fifteen, stolen by a friend from his mom's medicine cupboard. Within a couple of years, he had moved on to the prescription drug OxyContin, sometimes known as "hillbilly heroin." I worried about Adam—he'd been a good kid and I hated to see him lose his way like this. I felt sorry for his family, who'd done everything they could to raise him right and give him a good life. Trying to help him out, in 2010 I offered him a job at the dealership doing oil changes. Unfortunately, his continuing drug use compromised his ability to work. We fired him, then rehired him, then fired him again, and eventually he drifted away.

The next thing I heard was when his brother told me that Adam was living rough in San Francisco's infamous Tenderloin District, hooked on heroin. He later told me that he'd moved on to heroin because it was cheaper than OxyContin and easy to come by on San Francisco's "Pill Hill," as the corner of Golden Gate and Leavenworth is known. His parents were heartbroken— his mom was fighting a life-threatening illness, their oldest son was a long-time meth addict, and now Adam was a homeless heroin junkie. Feeling their pain, I agreed to go over to the city and look for him.

Several times, I drove over the Bay Bridge and walked those streets, peering under the hoodies and blankets of homeless men, seeking a glimpse of his freckled face and red hair. That was a pretty scary experience, and I had no luck finding him. As the weeks and months passed, I often thought of him out there on the streets, especially when it was cold out.

Finally, one night in early 2012, I posted a message on his Facebook page: "Adam, I need to talk to you." I didn't know if it would reach him, but it turned out he was still going to the business center of a nearby hotel and checking his messages once a week. I prayed, and waited, hoping he would call. This may sound a little crazy, but I also had gotten into the habit of asking Margot's spirit to help me with issues like this. I often felt her presence and her wisdom guiding my actions—I still do. She'd known Adam when he worked at the dealership and had tried to help him, rooting for the underdog as she always did. So each morning when I was writing in my journal and taking quiet time for prayer and reflection, I asked her to have Adam call me.

About a week after I'd posted the message on Facebook, for some strange reason, I felt compelled to watch the video of Margot's memorial service—something I had not done in six months or so. Just as the video was ending, Adam called, reaching out for my help. Later he told me that his heart had jumped when he saw my message. Somehow he knew I was offering a way out, and he was ready. After Adam and I spoke, I called my sons—Chris and Mike—and they dropped everything to come with me. We jumped in the car and drove across the bridge, cruising through parts of town where you never want to go alone. We waited about half an hour on the street in the freezing cold, surrounded by young heroin addicts, before Adam showed up—haggard and high, looking a decade older than when I'd last seen him just a couple years before. We bundled him into the car and drove him across the bay to my son's house, and I booked him on a 6:00 a.m. flight to the rehab center in Iowa.

I've never been more proud of the fine men my sons have become than I was that night. If I could leave no other legacy, I'd feel happy just knowing that I helped to bring them into this world. While I grabbed a couple of hours of sleep, they stayed up all night with their childhood friend as he went in and out of a heroin-induced stupor. Adam remembers little of that night or the early-dawn ride to the airport, while Chris worried he might stop breathing and Mike was too concerned to sleep, even after being up all night.

Unfortunately, we missed the flight. We headed back to my house, exhausted. While I caught a little more sleep, my son Mike stayed with Adam and found him a medical detox facility in nearby Concord. Mike and Chris drove him there that afternoon. The kindness, compassion, and love they showed for their friend touched me deeply.

After spending a few days at the Concord facility, Adam flew to Iowa and spent two months in the rehab program. During his time there, he started writing poetry, finding it a powerful outlet for his inner voice. His first poem, addressed to his drug of choice, began, "Heroin, heroin, I have to say goodbye." It's a bit too profanity-laced to reprint here in full, but I love the poem—curse words and all—and I have it hanging on my fridge to this day. I'll share a couple of lines to give you a sense of its raw authenticity:

> *I thought you were the love of my life,*
> *You bitch, I even called you my wife.*
> *It's time I step up and get up on my horse,*
> *I think it's time we get a divorce.*
> *For so long you made me blame others,*
> *And now it's time I get back to my brothers.*

Adam successfully completed rehab, where they taught him, he told me, to live life successfully and to stop running from his problems. He was able to say goodbye to the dope because, as he wrote at the end of the poem, "I've got something new called faith, love, and hope." For a kid who'd failed so many times in his attempts to quit drugs, finally gaining some confidence in his own ability to beat his addiction meant everything. Now he's been months in a sober-living facility back in Walnut Creek and is working for us again as a mechanic. The shadows have gone from his face, and I can now see the resemblance to the little boy in the framed theme park photograph.

"Every day use your magic to be of service to others."

—Marcia Wieder

A Mom's Prayer Answered

While Adam was finishing up rehab, I got a call from Nick's mom, Nancy, in Ohio. Nick had relapsed and was back in jail. Saddened to hear this, I sent her Adam's poem, and in response, she wrote me a very moving letter, and included a poem of her own:

A Mom's Prayer

Goodbye heroin,
It's time for you to go.
You snuck into our lives.
How? I'll never know.

Ever so quietly,
There you were.
And now here we are,
It's all such a blur.

You told my son
How great he would feel.

You forgot to say
It was always your deal.

So quickly you slipped
Your noose around his neck.
Pulling it tighter
With each hit he took.

Pretty soon,
The high was not the same.
Now he needs you daily,
It's always been your game.

At first you felt great,
That's what I've been told.
Then all HELL breaks loose,
AND THE HIGH JUST GETS OLD.

So many people,
So many lives,
Have fallen into your grips,
So only you could thrive.

Not only is the addicted affected,
But everyone around.
Our lives have been ruined,
But we will rebound!

My boy is stronger than you,
Just so you know.
He is a better person,
Because GOD tells me so.
So get out of our lives
And leave others alone.
You're not what you promised,
Your story has flown.

If I sound like I'm pleading,
And asking you sweetly,
You couldn't be more wrong.
I'm screaming . . . RELEASE ME!

GOD is stronger than you,
That's one thing I know,
So goodbye heroin,
I'm done feeling low.

At the time of this writing, Nick has been through rehab again and has been clean for many months. I hope and pray he will win the fight this time. It breaks my heart to think how many good kids and loving families are affected by the horrors of drug addiction. As Nick's mom wrote in her letter of thanks to the foundation, "Addiction knows no economic or demographical limits. It can happen to anyone." It's a problem our society hasn't begun to tackle. And while my primary calling, at this point in my life, is to serve those with life-threatening diseases in Margot's memory, I am grateful that I had the opportunity to make a difference in the lives of these two young men who had lost their way. There may be tens of thousands more starfish on the beach, but these two are swimming again.

"When love exists, nothing else matters, not life's predicaments, not the fury of the years, not a physical winding down or scarcity of opportunity."
—Isabel Allende,
Aphrodite

Why I'm Hopeful

I told Adam the story of the boy and the starfish

179

when I saw him recently. He thanked me for everything I'd done for him, and I told him that all I asked in return was that he become stable in his recovery and that he find a way each day to do something for someone else with a loving, open heart. A couple of days later, I saw a post on his Facebook page that brought a smile to my face. It was just two words: "Another starfish." To me, this means more than all the gratitude in the world—to know that someone who at one point could not even help himself is now making the effort to give and to serve in whatever ways he can.

People often ask me how I can sustain my energy for doing good when the scale of the problems confronting us is so overwhelming. Because we are all connected, and the energy of our connectedness is love, there is no limit to the impact we can have when we help one person. If, by helping another, we not only put that person on a better path but also awaken in his or her heart a compassionate desire to serve, we are setting in motion a chain reaction of love. Yes, there is much suffering and pain in the world, but I firmly believe there is more love.

If we can choose love over fear, we will embrace life with all it brings us. First, we must learn to embrace and love ourselves, in all our imperfection. Then we can learn to love others, to give love unfiltered by fear. The best news is that love is contagious. When we experience true love from another person, it has the power to melt our fear and inspire us to love more. That's why I have high hopes for a better world every time I see another face light up when touched by Margot's love through the work of the foundation, and I know that that person will go out into the world with a more open heart and a desire to give back.

Adam's Angel

Adam recently shared with me another poem that he wrote while in rehab. "The rehab folks were always telling me God was looking out for me," he said. "But I wasn't really big on God. As far as I was concerned, it was you who saved me. Then I told them the story about Margot, and I realized that's who's looking out for me. She saved my life—through you." I'll end with Adam's poem, because it captures so beautifully the essence of Margot's love. Every word he writes could be my own:

Margot, I truly believe you're my angel and came down to save my soul,
And helping many others in need because that's your goal.
We might not see you but we know you are there,
Floating and twirling in the crisp winter air,
You were always there for me in my toughest of times,
And did not judge me when I committed crimes.
You were always so happy and had a big old smile,
And always looked so beautiful because you had great style.
You are always there and always in my heart,
Wait, who am I kidding? You have been since the start.
Thank you so much for never giving up on me and being my friend.
I know you will have my back till the very end.
My dreams, wishes, and prayers are finally coming true.
Thanks for being my angel—just want to say
I love you.

EPILOGUE
Margot's Legacy

Not long before Margot died, she was rushed by ambulance to the hospital. We had just moved back to Northern California the week before Memorial Day, and we didn't even have a new oncologist yet. (I had fired the one we'd been working with because I didn't like the way his staff treated Margot.) Now Margot had woken up in such extreme pain that we had to call 911. As we raced to the hospital, I

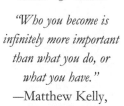

"Who you become is infinitely more important than what you do, or what you have."
—Matthew Kelly,
The Rhythm of Life

frantically searched for a new doctor. I finally reached someone who had been recommended to us, and thankfully he promised he would meet us later that day.

We arrived at the hospital, went through the ER procedures, and finally Margot was settled in a room. For the first time in the past seven months, there were just her closest family members around her—her mother and father, her sister Lola, and myself. The only other great love of her life, her boxer Duke, was waiting at home.

The doctor arrived, and after hearing a brief overview of Margot's case and reviewing her charts, he asked us right out if we'd discussed end-of-life procedures. He struck me as forthright but also soft—a good combination in a doctor. He wanted to hear from Margot, and she bravely answered his questions. When she'd finished, he said, "I have to be honest with you. It's Thursday, and this weekend is Memorial Day. The chemo drugs you need are hard to get hold of, and if I can't get them tomorrow, before the holiday weekend, you'll be dead within a few days."

I couldn't even pause to let in what he'd said. "Well, you'd better go find the chemo," I told him in typically blunt fashion.

After he left the room, it was just the five of us— Margot and the people she loved most in the world. Her mother, Martha, a deceptively small and sweet Peruvian woman who is actually a tower of strength, took a deep breath and asked her daughter, "Margot, what do you want from each of us for the rest of our lives?"

Margot, as always, was full of grace and bravery. She was the only one in the room not in tears. I was in a state of shock, reeling from the reality that after all these years of fighting, I might be so close to losing the love of my life. But she didn't stop to process the information, nor did she waste one precious moment fighting with reality. While all of us were drowning in emotion, she seemed able to rise above it, without fear or sadness. She held a meeting with us all, with the authority of a Fortune 500 CEO, going around the room one at a time and telling each of us how she wanted us to live. She seemed determined not to let anything be left unsaid for another day, just in case it would turn out to be her last.

I don't remember much of what was said, but her sister Lola remembers more of the detail and the quality of that extraordinary gathering. She described feeling stripped bare, as if everyone in the room had become transparent. "There was nothing between us," she recalled.

Margot spoke first to her father, who was not a religious man and was struggling with his own health challenges. "I want you to find God," she told him. To Lola, she said, "Don't be sad. Continue to be an amazing mother to your kids. You don't have to be perfect." I do remember her telling her mom to find time to travel and not to be sad. And she said four words to me that I've never forgotten: "Be a good man!"

Only because she came into my life, and loved me the way that she did, do I feel that there is some hope that before I pass on from this earth, I can fulfill her dying wish for me. Her legacy is many things—the people whose lives she touched, the work of the foundation, the lessons shared in this book, the love that our clients feel in the practical support we give them. But I also feel that I am her legacy. She made me who I am—transformed me into the best part of myself. That is the responsibility I feel when I wake up each day and strive to be of service, to be a good man. If I can carry forward even a fraction of the love and light she brought into this world, my life will have been worthwhile.

In some small way, each one of us is the legacy of those who moved on before us—those whose love and care and wisdom shaped and nurtured us. I hope that as you close this book and go out into this world, it will kindle in your heart a deep gratitude for the love you have been given, and a desire to make your life a monument to the glory of that love.

The Love From Margot Foundation

The Love from Margot Foundation was created in memory of Margot Murphy. The foundation began serving clients informally in January 2012, and since then it has worked with more than thirty people in the Bay Area, helping them meet their financial obligations while battling the physical and emotional effects of a serious illness. In addition, the foundation has partnered with the Shanti Project in San Francisco, Highland Hospital in Oakland, and Gilda's Club in Palm Desert, California, to help hundreds more.

In order that 100 percent of donations will go directly to clients, founder Mike Murphy covers all overhead and expenses of running the programs. If you would like to learn more about the foundation and read the stories of the people we've helped, please visit www.lovefrommargot.com.

Endnotes

1 Max Planck, "Das Wesen der Materie" [The Nature of Matter], speech, Florence, Italy, 1944, Archiv zur Geschichte der Max-Planck-Gesellschaft, Abt. Va. Rep 11 Planck, Nr. 1797.

2 Prentice Mulford, *Thoughts Are Things,* (Frontal Lobe Publishing, April 22, 2011) p. 116.

3 Wayne Dyer, from a talk at Wanderlust California Yoga Festival, July 2012, reported in *Wanderlust Journal* 4/19/13: http://journal.wanderlustfestival.com/connect/blog/wayne-dyer-master-art-manifesting#sthash.XM380aEA.dpuf. Accessed August 2013.

4 Albert Einstein, letter to the family of his lifelong friend Michele Besso after learning of his death (March 1955), as quoted in Kowalski, Gary A., *Science and the Search for God* (Lantern Books, 2003) p. 24.

5 Woody Allen, *Without Feathers* (Ballantine Books; First Edition, February 12, 1986) p. 109.

6 Daniel Gilbert, *Stumbling on Happiness* (Vintage Books, 2007) p. xiii-xiv.

7 ibid, p. xiv.

8 Thich Nhat Hanh, *Teachings on Happiness,* (Parallax Press, 2009) p. 53.

9 Marci Shimoff, *Happy For No Reason* (Atria Books, March 3, 2009) p. 29.

10 Stephen G. Post, "Altruism, Happiness, and Health: It's Good to Be Good," International Journal of Behavioral Medicine Vol. 12, No. 2, 66–77.

11 Rosabeth Moss Kanter, "The Happiest People Pursue the Most Difficult Problems," Harvard Business Review Blog Network, April 10, 2013, http://blogs.hbr.org/kanter/2013/04/to-find-happiness-at-work-tap.html. Accessed August 2013.

12 Arianna Huffington, Smith College Commencement Speech: "Redefining Success: The Third Metric,"

http://www.huffingtonpost.com/2013/05/19/arianna-huffington-smith-college-commencement-speech_n_3299888.html. Accessed August 2013.

[13] Jeffrey Gitterman, *Beyond Success* (AMACOM, 2009) p. 144.

[14] Louis C.K., "Another Statement from Louis C.K.," December 21, 2011, https://buy.louisck.net/news/another-statement-from-louis-c-k. Accessed August 2013.

[15] Quoted in Edward Hoffman, *The Right to Be Human: A Biography of Abraham Maslow,* (McGraw-Hill, 1999) p. 143.

[16] Carl Jung, *Modern Man In Search of a Soul* (Harcourt Harvest, 1955), p. 49.

[17] Debbie Ford, Deepak Chopra, and Marianne Williamson, *The Shadow Effect* (HarperCollins, 2010) p. 2.

[18] ibid, p. 2.

[19] Robert Augustus Masters, "Bringing Your Shadow Out of the Dark" (April 2013) on *Integral Post*: http://integrallife.com/integral-post/bringing-your-shadow-out-dark#sthash.o5QkLNNT.dpuf. Accessed August 2013.

[20] Marianne Williamson, *A Return To Love*, (HarperOne, Reissue edition, March 15, 1996) p. xx.

[21] Bill Watterson, *The Essential Calvin and Hobbes*, (Andrews McMeel Publishing, January 1, 1988) p. 100.

[22] Bronnie Ware, "Top 5 Regrets of the Dying," on Huffington Post, January 21, 2012: http://www.huffingtonpost.com/bronnie-ware/top-5-regrets-of-the-dyin_b_1220965.html. Accessed August 2013.

[23] Byron Katie, *Loving What Is* (Harmony, December 23, 2003) p. 2–3.

[24] ibid, p. 3

[25] "What is Spiritual Healing? An Interview with Dale Borglum" on Seven Ponds: http://blog.sevenponds.com/professional-advice/an-interview-with-dale-borglum#sthash.zGUrQP9H.dpuf. Accessed August 2013.

[26] C.S. Lewis, *A Grief Observed,* (HarperCollins, Mar 29, 1989) p. 15.

[27] Byron Katie, *Loving What Is* (Harmony, December 23, 2003) p. 211.

[28] Ram Dass, *Still Here (*Riverhead Books, June 1, 2001) p. 201.

[29] Byron Katie, *Loving What Is* (Harmony, December 23, 2003) p. 216.

[30] Roy F. Baumeister, Florida State University; Kathleen D. Vohs, University of Minnesota; Jennifer L. Aaker, Stanford University; Emily N. Garbinsky, Stanford University; "Some Key Differences between a Happy Life and a Meaningful Life," published at: http://faculty-gsb.stanford.edu/aaker/pages/documents/SomeKeyDifferencesHappyLifeMeaningfulLife_2012.pdf. Accessed August 2013.

[31] Victor Frankl, *Man's Search for Ultimate Meaning* (Basic Books, July 2000) p. 90.

[32] Victor Frankl, *Man's Search for Meaning* (Beacon Press, June 1, 2006) p. 88.

[33] *ibid* p.12.

[34] *ibid* p. 115.

[35] Lynne Twist, *The Soul of Money,* (W.W. Norton, 2006) p. 8.

[36] David Wagner, *Life as a Daymaker* (Jodere Group, Oct 1, 2002) p. 3.

[37] Jack Kornfield, *Buddha's Little Instruction Book,* (Bantam, May 1, 1994) p. 28.

[38] Brian Tracy, *The Way to Wealth Pt. II,* (Entrepreneur Press, 2007) p. 219.

[39] *The Dhammapada*, translated by Ananda Maitreya (Parallax Press, Aug 1, 1995) p. 2.

[40] David Godman, *Be As You Are: The Teachings of Ramana Maharshi* (Penguin Books, February 1, 1989) p. 59.

[41] Aldous Huxley, *The Perennial Philosophy* (Harper Perennial Modern Classics, July 28, 2009) p. 5.

[42] Albert Einstein, Letter to Robert S. Marcus, February 12,

1950, in *Dear Professor Einstein,* Ed. Alice Calaprice (New York: Prometheus Books, 2002) p. 184.

⁴³ M. Scott Peck, *The Road Less Traveled* (Touchstone, Anniversary Edition, February 4, 2003) p. 15.

⁴⁴ Carl Sagan, *Cosmos* (New York: Random House, 1980), p. 193.

⁴⁵ Stephen Jay Gould, *The Panda's Thumb* (W. W. Norton & Company, August 17, 1992) p. 302.

⁴⁶ Joel Primack and Nancy Abrams, *View From the Center of the Universe* (Riverhead Trade, August 7, 2007) p. 151.

⁴⁷ Carl Sagan, *Cosmos,* Episode 13, "Who Speaks for Earth?" (PBS, 1990).

⁴⁸ Pierre Teilhard de Chardin, *The Future of Man* (Image, April 2004) p. 7.

⁴⁹ John Muir, journal entry for July 27, 1869, quoted in Stephen Fox, *John Muir and His Legacy* (Little, Brown and Company, 1981) p. 291.